PRAISE FOR Christ Before Creeds

CW01032834

"In this century, we have witnessed foundations of trinitarian doctrine. Jeff Deuble's *Christ Before Creeds*. To biblical depth and an exceptionally necessary, yet is always warm and irer and historical data is even-handed and engaging, never tedious or ... Anyone who is a thinker—whether trinitarian or non-trinitarian—and who has a concern for the biblical truth about Jesus Christ, will welcome this fine book."

—Bentley C. F. Chan, author of *Theological Metamorphosis* and secondary author of *The Only Perfect Man: The Glory of God in the Face of Jesus Christ*

"Not all irritants are prophets, but certainly all prophets are irritants. In this prophetic tradition, Jeff Deuble calls us to re-examine our fundamental beliefs and rediscover the Jesus of history, in whose footsteps we follow. Jeff points to an authentic Jesus who can't be sung to sleep or contained in a creed; his careful argument is built on his own robust faith. Good will come from the dialogue this book will generate."

—Graham Long, pastor emeritus of The Wayside Chapel in Sydney, Australia, author of *Love Over Hate: Finding Life By The Wayside*

"In the first six chapters of *Christ before Creeds*, Jeff Deuble does a great job of cutting through the fog of theological speculation and church tradition to get to the heart of the biblical proclamation of who God and Messiah are. Christian and non-Christian alike will be challenged by this book."

—Bill Schlegel, author of *The Satellite Bible Atlas*, host of the One God Report podcast

"Deuble has accomplished something quite rare in *Christ Before Creeds*. He has taken a long misunderstood area of Christian faith and given the church a gentle and loving challenge to rethink whether the Trinity is a scriptural way to view our God. He has made a clear and compelling presentation of Jesus as our Messiah and the Father as our one true God and has helped clarify their relationship to each other—and to all of us as well. Jeff Deuble brings to his work both a teacher's eye and a pastor's heart. The result is a work both biblically sound and lovingly accessible. Christ Before Creeds is a welcome addition to the study of God and His wonderful son."

—Robert Carden, author of *One God: The Unfinished Reformation*

"Jeff has taken a courageous step in writing this book in which he re-examines his own theological beliefs as a veteran pastor concerning the Trinity. He shows great humility by reconsidering what the Bible says on its own merits rather than relying on creeds and religious traditions. As you follow his journey of discovery, you will appreciate his straightforward and well reasoned writing style. He lays out what the Bible teaches about Christ in a logical and clear way that readers will easily understand, and he reaches some astounding conclusions that will push you to think deeply. For anyone with questions about who Christ is and the doctrine of the trinity, this is a must read."

—Seth Ross, Executive Director of the Church of God
General Conference and President of
Atlanta Bible College

"...Our author is neither sectarian nor self-righteous. He argues for unity, not division, humility, not pride, dialogue, not mutual demonization, and peace, not theological war. This book advocates both the teaching and the spirit of our Lord Jesus Christ. By God's grace, may both prevail among us as we continue the important task of scriptural Reformation."

—Dale Tuggy (PhD, Brown University), host of the Trinities podcast,
author of *What is the Trinity?*, co-author of *Is Jesus Human and Not Divine?*,
Chair of the Board of the Unitarian Christian Alliance

"'He who shows me where I err is not my enemy, he is my friend!' If that adage is true, then Jeff Deuble should become the friend of many through this book. Jeff invites his readers to introspection and reconsideration of great issues. But he does so only after having set the example of doing that himself. I can say by personal experience that reconsidering our cherished beliefs is a hard thing to do no matter what our religious backgrounds may be. Yet, doing so helps to clear the way for a sounder, more wonderful faith. We can have a faith that is more scriptural, more pleasing to God, beneficial to ourselves and that makes more sense to the world we seek to reach."

—J. Dan Gill, editor-in-chief of 21st Century Reformation

Christ Before Creeds
Rediscovering the Jesus of History

By Jeff Deuble, DipTh, BA, DMin

"Just because our tradition tells us that the Bible says and means one thing or another, that does not excuse us from the challenging task of studying it afresh in the light of the best knowledge we have about its world and context, to see whether these things are indeed so."

— *N.T. Wright*

Cover design by Glenn Newton
Cover image: Ali Rizwan
Book design by Anna Shoffner Brown and Paola Ely

Paperback ISBN: 978-1-7369180-1-2
e-book ISBN: 978-1-7369180-0-5

www.christbeforecreeds.com

Acknowledgments

I wish to acknowledge my indebtedness to all who have contributed and assisted significantly in the writing of this book. Specifically, I express my sincere gratitude and deepest thanks to...

Sean Finnegan, who believed in the value of this book, for his kind support and wonderful encouragement, and to Living Hope International Ministries for their sponsorship of this book's publication.

Anna Brown, who has proofread, edited and managed this book's production with incredible grace, diligence, enthusiasm, and professionalism. Her value add to my initial manuscript has been amazing.

Paola Ely, who has given valuable assistance with her formatting and graphic design work. I thank her for her expert input and incredible helpfulness.

Dr. Dale Tuggy, for the generosity of his time and effort in providing comprehensive feedback and helpful suggestions on the content.

Professor Richard Rubenstein, for reading the book and writing the Foreword, his positive appraisal and genuine, gracious comments.

I also want to acknowledge the huge formative influence and ongoing wonderful support of family members into my life and work, including...

> My grandfather, who instilled in me a love for God and his word.

My mother, who nurtured me in my spiritual development through the example and inspiration of her heart, faith, and life.

My brother, who continues to give encouragement and insight to spur my understanding of the Scriptures.

My wife—I could not have wished for a more wonderful, loving partner and supportive companion.

My sons and their wives, who continue to care for and support me, even though they have had to bear some unfortunate consequences of my unorthodox views.

Ultimately, I give all credit, thanks and praise to my glorious God and loving Heavenly Father through his beloved Son, my Lord and Savior, Jesus the Messiah.

"A man should look for what is, and not for what he thinks should be."

— *Albert Einstein*

CONTENTS

FOREWORD

I was eager to read an advance copy of Pastor Jeff Deuble's *Christ Before Creeds* because we share a common interest. I understood that his book focused on the question of trinitarianism, a topic on which I had written years ago, and which still interests me greatly. My historical survey, *When Jesus Became God*, was an account of the ancient struggle to define the relationship of the Son to the Father later known as the Arian controversy. It was not intended to affirm or deny the doctrine of the three-personed God, but rather to explain how and why some religious disputes become lethal. In the fourth century, what some might consider an abstruse theological debate became a long, bloody struggle that ended only when the belief that "the Son was God" was declared orthodox and non-trinitarianism became a heresy punishable by death.

After that book was published, I had the opportunity to speak in many Christian churches and discovered, to my surprise, that controversy about the Trinity was very much alive, even among the members of nominally trinitarian congregations. A wide variety of believers came to tell that, despite their daily or weekly recitation of the Nicene Creed, the Apostles' Creed, or other statements of "orthodox" belief, they either did not understand the meaning of the credo, affirmed the Trinity in some purely metaphorical sense, or disbelieved the doctrine outright. Jeff Deuble's stimulating discussion provides further evidence that this search for meaning is still with us—indeed, that the discussion may even be entering a new phase of contention.

I say this understanding that *Christ Before Creeds*, although vigorously argued, is not "contentious" in a sense that, rightfully, turns many people off to cocksure and intolerant expressions of opinion. There are three reasons, in particular, to read and ponder this carefully reasoned and appealing study:

The first is that Jeff's book is written in a style that I would call elegantly simple. Even when analyzing complex questions, his writing is crystal clear, personally voiced, direct, lively…and never "preachy." Lengthier discussions of biblical passages are reserved for appendices that leave the main part of the text refreshingly free of exegetical calisthenics. Moreover, even the appendices are readable! As a result, this is a briskly paced, unusually enjoyable "read" that naturally inspires the reader to share and discuss its ideas with others.

Second, in its structure and mode of argument, this presentation is a model of persuasiveness. The book's first three chapters ("Why This Book?", "Why Bother?", and "Why Question?") draw the reader step by step into considering and reconsidering his or her beliefs concerning the Father's oneness and the Son's unique role. The final four chapters ("What Went Wrong?", "What Does the Bible Teach?", "Who Is Jesus?", and "What's Essential?") deliver the substantive goods. I will have more to say in a moment about the major arguments made here, but it is important to note that the book's persuasiveness also rests on its thoroughness and its honest style of argument. The author does not "cherry pick" biblical texts and other evidence in the legalistic manner of so many polemical writers. He presents all the texts and evidence relevant to the issues discussed, including material that some might consider adverse to his position, and deals with this material calmly and fairly. The result is to build trust between himself and his readers.

Third, while clearly advocating his own non-trinitarian point of view, the author clearly disclaims any intention to judge readers harshly who disagree with him. His arguments are intended to convince, not to "convert" those who may not have come to the same conclusions as he has about challenging issues of belief. As a teacher of conflict resolution, I find myself sympathizing profoundly with Jeff's declaration that his primary purpose is to establish the legitimacy of the discussion and eliminate labels such as "heretic," rather than to win a debate. His appeal for mutually respectful discussion, and his enumeration of the principles that may provide a basis for Christian unity despite disagreements about trinitarianism, are both sensible and moving.

When it comes to the major arguments presented to counter commonly accepted views of the Trinity, the author makes several points that seem difficult, if not impossible, to refute. To begin with, he states correctly that the belief that Jesus was God in the flesh rather than a uniquely holy—but entirely human—Messiah was an innovation that took almost four centuries to establish as official Church doctrine. He accurately describes a process by which Christian leaders turned away from their (and Jesus's) Hebraic roots in order to embrace a concept of the Godhead rooted in Greek philosophical traditions rather than in Scripture. Among the most revealing and persuasive parts of this presentation are his discussions of Jewish concepts of agency, preexistence, and words describing deity, all of which strongly support the idea that trinitarianism is a later development not validated by either the Old Testament or the Gospels.

Jeff's discussion of biblical texts, including such allegedly trinitarian "proof texts" as "I and the Father are one," seems to me equally persuasive, since it is based on a solid understanding of the meaning of such words to first- and second-century Jewish Christians. The climax of the book, however, takes place after this clearing away of misconceptions has been done. This is the author's affirmation that defining Jesus as a uniquely holy, divinely chosen person rather than the second person of a trinity does not make him any less worth glorifying and following, but actually clarifies and intensifies the Christian believer's relationship to him as Messiah, Lord, and Savior.

Even an outsider to Christianity, like this writer, can appreciate the power of this affirmation as well as the author's sincerity and faith. He consistently asks those who may be reciting words as part of their religious practice to think about what the words mean and to turn belief into action. One can only hope that his appeal for humane and respectful discussion of these difficult and important issues will inspire others to respond in the same spirit.

—Richard E. Rubenstein
university professor, George Mason University
author of *When Jesus Became God: The Struggle to Define Christianity During the Last Days of Rome*

Chapter 1

Why This Book?

I clearly recall the moment when, as a young boy on our Easter vacation, I discovered a large shopping bag full of Easter eggs. With that discovery it dawned on me that the senior members of my family had deceived me about the Easter bunny. I remember how angry and upset I was at the time when I realized that the truth had been hidden from me. But as I worked through that initial shock and disappointment, I came to appreciate that even though some of the embellishments around Easter were wrong, the central truths of Jesus' death and resurrection were very real and significant.

Years later, around Christmas, a similar disenchantment happened. I had grown up with the traditional narrative and typical nativity scene in my mind concerning the birth of Jesus. But I began to realize that this "orthodox" version, accepted by virtually everyone, did not align accurately with the Bible story. There is no mention that Mary rode a donkey. The magi were not present with the shepherds at the birth of Jesus. They arrived some time later when Jesus was an infant (Greek: *paidion*), about 18 months old. Even the stable behind the inn was probably a living area shared with animals (Greek: *kataluma*) in the home of a relative.[1]

Again, coming to terms with those misrepresentations did not ultimately detract from the wonder and significance of the birth of a Savior, God's gift given in love and goodwill to the world.

More recently I have embarked on a similar journey of discovery,

1. For a full discussion of this topic, see Kenneth E. Bailey, *Jesus Through Middle Eastern Eyes: Cultural Studies in the Gospels* (Downers Grove, IL: InterVarsity Press, 2008).

disorientation, and re-establishment of faith—this time over the nature and person of Jesus. I grew up, as most Christians, with a Trinitarian understanding of God, Jesus, and the Holy Spirit. Then I came across new information that seriously challenged my understanding about the interrelationship between these three and the orthodox view that is generally accepted and taught concerning Jesus.

While initially troubling, as I have had time to process this new information, I have found it has not destroyed, but only served to further develop and deepen my faith in Christ. I believe I now have a more biblically accurate, more intellectually congruent, more historically authentic, and more personally fulfilling understanding of who Jesus is.

This book is written with a desire that you, too, will discover the authentic Jesus of the Scriptures, as opposed to a Jesus of Greek mystical or philosophical construction, as expressed in later church creeds.

I want to make clear from the outset that, despite my passion to uphold and protect the integrity of Jesus and the biblical witness as to who he is and how he lived, the primary aim of this book is not to win a theological argument. It is not to prove my position right and opposing views wrong.

My intention is to impart information, create understanding, and build bridges. I want to appeal for Christian grace, for mutual acceptance and respect, for unity within the Body of Christ between those who share a Trinitarian belief in God and those who don't. My plea echoes that of the Apostle Paul: "Make every effort to keep the unity of the Spirit through the bond of peace" (Eph. 4:3).[2]

Historically, there has always existed a deep divide between opposing camps over the issue of the deity of Christ. Many today would still consider this a deal breaker in terms of the possibility of mutual acceptance or Christian fellowship. I will explain later why I

---

2. All biblical quotations are from the NIV unless otherwise noted. This is because it is widely used and regarded as having scholastic integrity (even though it does carry a Trinitarian bias in translation and interpretation).

believe such entrenched and adversarial positions are unfortunate and unnecessary.

But before we arrive at that part of the journey, I believe there may be some barriers that need to be confronted and overcome, such as...

- Apathy: Why does it matter? Who cares?
- Ignorance: I'm right, so don't confuse me with the facts.
- Pride or stubbornness: I'm right, and I won't be convinced otherwise.
- Self-preservation: It's too hard or costly to change.

How have we arrived at the present state of affairs, where Trinitarian doctrine possesses such prominence and dominance within Christendom? I will seek to answer this question in the early chapters, as well as address initial prejudices people often have. There is an informational, ideological power-imbalance on this issue, so I will seek to create a more level playing field.

Then there is the theological section, where the biblical case for a Non-trinitarian doctrine is presented. I seek to offer an alternative understanding from the one that is generally known and unquestioningly held. I think that to have integrity of belief, it's important to at least consider contrary evidence to one's position. Just as to hear only one side of the story is not to know the whole story, I believe if you only know your side of the argument, you don't really know the argument.

Before we start, here are a few points, by way of explanation and clarification:

I acknowledge that this is a controversial and potentially touchy subject. For some, it seems to threaten the very core and foundation of their faith. Strong emotions are engaged, and typically a "fight or flight" response kicks in. I remember how defensive, upset, and angry I was when I first encountered a Non-trinitarian view that challenged "my Jesus" and, from my perspective at the time, sought to diminish his status and importance. But I believe that for Christians, the bottom line is that the truth has nothing to fear.

While I won't hold back from robust discussion or seeking to cogently present another point of view, please be assured my intention is to write with both grace and truth (John 1:17)—to challenge but not condemn, to invite reflection and review while maintaining respect, all the while extending the freedom for you to come to your own conclusions. It's in that spirit of openness, respect, and goodwill that I hope to engage your heart and mind in the coming chapters.

The approach is not overly academic or technical, but written with ordinary believers in mind. I do not want to comprehensively deal with every issue or passage of Scripture. There is a lot more depth and detail behind what is discussed here. (Some of which is presented in the Appendices.)

This book is an introduction for those who are open to search beyond the superficial. That's why I have attempted to strike a balance: simple, but not simplistic; neither technical nor trite.

Feel free to choose your level of reading:

Review: If you just want to get to the bottom line, you can read the summary statements at the end of chapters 1-5 and the whole of chapters 6 and 7.

Read: Read through from start to finish. This helps to fill in some of the background, providing reasons for the conclusions reached.

Research: I have decided to not include discussion around some of the more contentious passages in the main text, as it can get a little complicated or confusing. Instead, I have put this material in Appendix A. For those who want to explore further, there are some footnotes and also a list of resources for further investigation at the end, in Appendix B.

My approach is biblical rather than theological. You may wonder, "What's the difference?" Some may even challenge any distinction I may be suggesting between the two. While I appreciate the overlap and interplay between scriptural input and theological reflection, I maintain there is a significant difference—that being their respective approaches.

Theology, especially systematic theology, tends to begin with a cognitive structure—with categories, a framework, or a paradigm—and then searches and sorts biblical information accordingly. It may also start with an issue or question that is then addressed by referencing scriptural and other input.

The doctrine of the Trinity is largely a response to the question of how to align and fuse two seemingly mutually exclusive concepts: monotheism on one hand and the deity of Jesus on the other. However, even in the framing of this question certain assumptions are made that may or may not be biblical.

Many books written about the Trinity focus on quotes from scholars, theological interpretation and construction, philosophical reflection and argument, but not necessarily on biblical exegesis. They tend to start with a predetermined theological paradigm of God—three persons in one being—then select, interpret, and categorize biblical information accordingly.

But to start with the Bible is to allow the text to speak for itself in the first instance. It is to focus on exegesis, which is the practice and process whereby we study a passage of Scripture and seek to accurately understand its meaning. Exegesis asks: "What was the message the author sought to convey to his intended audience when he initially wrote the recorded words?"

This is in contrast to what is referred to as "eisegesis" where people read into the text what they want it to say—they interpret the words in a way that is biased or conforms to their personal assumptions and opinions. There is a discipline called hermeneutics which defines the methodology (principles and guidelines) that govern good exegesis and biblical interpretation.

As God's children, what can we rightly assume about the Bible? Can we trust that the words of our loving heavenly Father are not only true, but clear, coherent, congruent, and consistent? I believe so, and therefore my assumption is that the Bible is its own best commentary. The onus is on us to "correctly [handle] the word of truth"

(2 Tim. 2:15), taking into account everything God has revealed in the Scriptures, seeking to harmonize and refine insights gained collectively throughout the Bible. We shouldn't focus on certain Scriptures while downplaying or excluding others.

Underpinning all this is my conviction that "all Scripture is God-breathed and is useful for teaching, rebuking, correcting and training in righteousness, so that the servant of God may be thoroughly equipped for every good work" (2 Tim. 3:16-17). I believe that the Scriptures, as initially written in the original languages, are divinely trustworthy and authoritative in all things pertaining to our faith, life, and beliefs.

The bottom line is this: "I hold my Bible tightly, and my doctrine lightly." I will always seek to honor the Scriptures—to examine what I think or believe in light of what the Scriptures say. Because of this, if you believe I haven't interpreted a passage correctly, if you think my views are wrong or my understanding inadequate in some way, I invite your comment on my work.

Because of the entrenched overlays of ecclesiastical assumptions and interpretations—especially around the doctrine of the Trinity—I have spent a fair bit of time in the first few chapters doing some deconstruction. I beg your patience on this; I simply want to establish a firm foundation from which we can build. Also, towards the end I spend some time on application: if you reconstruct Jesus in a Non-trinitarian framework, what does that look like? And what does it mean for your faith and Christian life?

It may be helpful to clarify my usage of a few key terms:

Trinitarianism

This is the Christian doctrine that God exists as three distinct co-equal, co-eternal, consubstantial "persons" (Greek: *hypostases*): the Father, Son, and Holy Spirit. These three are one "being," sharing the same identical "essence" (*ousia*).[3]

There have been differing understandings, or schools of thought, as to how the three persons within the one being of God function and interrelate.

Some focus more on the three persons. The most commonly held view is Social Trinitarianism, which sees the persons of God as three distinct minds, centers of conscience and will that operate more like a group, a society of divine persons. The Trinity is therefore seen as expressing an interpersonal, loving relationship, and as such presents a positive model for human interaction and community—empathy, mutual belonging, and so forth. The challenge is how such a group can be called one "being." Is this simply tri-theism in denial?

Some focus more on the one being. The most common view is Latin Trinitarianism, inspired by Augustine and Aquinas, which sees God as three "event-based" persons who exist simultaneously—three facets or distinct parts of God's life always occurring at once, yet expressing themselves in different ways. While this preserves the monotheistic nature of God—his "oneness"—it struggles to escape the unorthodox Sabellian view (modalism) which sees God as one divine being who plays three different roles.

Monotheism

This is the doctrine or belief that there is only one God. This is accepted by both Trinitarians and Non-trinitarians as the biblical position; the point of departure is over the person and place of Jesus Christ. How does Jesus stand in relation to the Father? Is he fully equal, eternal, and co-essential with him, or different to and under him?

Once again, there are different schools of thought about the latter position. One is an "Arian" view that sees Jesus as the "first-

---

3. The third "person" of the Trinity is the Holy Spirit, who was actually added half a century after the Council of Nicea, around AD 381. The doctrine of the Holy Spirit will not be directly addressed in the discussion, but not because God's Spirit is unimportant. Teaching on God's Spirit is so crucial as to deserve a separate book on the subject. However, the fact is that considerations about the Spirit did not feature initially in the primary conflict at the time, which was essentially a Christological debate around the deity of Jesus.

fruits" of God's creation—a superior being, with whom and through whom the Father subsequently brought all other things into existence. The "Socinian" view (which I believe has strong scriptural support) is that Jesus is a human being, uniquely begotten of the Father, who although conceived in thought from the beginning of time, personally came to be at his birth in Bethlehem.

The Trinitarian challenge for both views is whether they fully account for what the Bible testifies about Jesus' exalted position and relationship with the Father.

Unitarianism

You will note that I steer away from using this term, mainly because of some of the negative baggage it carries. As an organized church, Unitarianism grew out of the Protestant Reformation in Europe in the sixteenth century. Its more recent iteration in the United States not only abandoned the doctrine of the Trinity, but became, among other things, very liberal, humanistic, and universalist in outlook. To avoid these negative associations, some use the term "Biblical Monotheism" to distinguish their position. But Trinitarians would claim that this term also expresses their belief. Hence, I am using the label "Non-trinitarian" to designate a view contrary from the "orthodox" one when it comes to theology and Christology.

Divine

This word is of Latin rather than Hebrew or Greek origin. Its traditional meaning is simply to be like God, pertaining to God, godly or godlike. In this sense, Jesus is divine (John 10:30; 14:9; Col. 1:15; Heb. 3:1). But then, Jesus said other people are as well (John 10:34). Paul says we are the "image and glory of God" (1 Cor. 11:7), and Peter says that we "participate in the divine nature" (2 Pet. 1:4). So there is a sense in which we, also, are divine or godlike, and hopefully becoming increasingly so through the sanctifying work of the Holy Spirit: "being transformed into his image with ever-increasing glory" (2 Cor. 3:18).

Deity

On the other hand, "deity" is having the rank and essence of God, or a god. It is to actually be God in person. For example, Paul is happy to say that Christ is "divine"—he is "of God" (1 Cor. 3:23), in "the image of God" (2 Cor. 4:4), "the Son of God" (2 Cor. 1:19), he is at the right hand of God, with all things subject to him (Eph. 1:20-23)—but does he ever deify Jesus and say *he is actually God?* That's a question we will consider later, but at this stage the distinction is a significant one to introduce.

Nature

The problem with this word in our English vocabulary is that it can mean either our inner essence, that which distinguishes us from other creatures in kind (our "human nature"), or it can mean those characteristics that we possess in temperament, personality, attitude, and so forth, that set us apart from others of our own kind—e.g., "she has a loving and gracious nature." The first is about our ontology (being) the second about our character (heart). When we say that Jesus has a divine nature, in what sense do we mean it?

As you've probably started to realize, things can get a bit technical. But I believe if we can get back to the basics, to what the Bible actually teaches, rather than getting caught up in theological deliberation or philosophical speculation, there is less chance of us getting off track. As you continue reading, my prayer is that of Paul's for the Ephesians: "I keep asking that the God of our Lord Jesus Christ, the glorious Father, may give you the Spirit of wisdom and revelation, so that you may know him better" (Eph. 1:17).

Summary:

This book is an invitation to re-examine what the Bible actually teaches about who Jesus is and how he lived. Trinitarian orthodoxy will not be assumed, but evaluated historically and scripturally to see if this theological construct aligns with what the original writers of the Old and New Testaments actually believed and taught.

CHAPTER 2

WHY BOTHER?

FOR THE FIRST 48 YEARS of my life, I was a committed Trinitarian. I was taught it, I believed it, and I had no reason to question it. As a pastor, I preached it from the pulpit. Then one day my older brother Greg confided in me that he no longer believed in the Trinity. He had come to a different understanding of Jesus.

I was shocked. In fact, I still remember my visceral reaction to some of his initial statements. When he said, "I believe Jesus is the Son of God, but not God the Son," I felt quite sick.

Had it been anyone other than my brother who had made such comments, I would have dismissed them out of hand. But I knew Greg's heart for God, his commitment to Jesus, and his biblical knowledge and love of the Scriptures. I was baffled. My major goal in our initial discussions was to seek to bring him back to his senses, arguing him back into orthodox faith. I remember quoting some of the texts that I believed taught Jesus was fully God and reiterating arguments I had always used to defend my position on the Trinity.

Those initial conversations were candid and robust. After a while I began to realize that this doctrine was not as clear cut as I had thought. In fact, there was much of which I was totally unaware. So began a journey over a number of years where I re-examined my theology and Christology, asking: what does the Bible actually teach about who God is and about the person and nature of Jesus?

I freely admit that my interest was piqued, and my motivation fuelled, by my brother's change in position, which then challenged my own. Otherwise I would have had no need or desire to embark on something so confusing, risky, and isolating.

Which leads me to ask the question: Why would the average Christian who has been schooled in Trinitarian doctrine want to re-examine their understanding of the nature and interrelationship between Father, Son, and Holy Spirit? Why bother? There are so many reasons *not* to:

- It is confusing.
- It is time-consuming.
- It is destabilizing—it could upset the apple cart.
- Practically, there seems little to gain.
- It is isolating—you'll probably lose some friends and make some enemies.
- It has the potential to cause angst, conflict, and division.

There are tacit assumptions people hold which can hinder their authentic exploration of this issue. Typically, people will adopt one of the following four positions. You may find yourself identifying with one or more of them:

It's Clear Cut

Some already have an entrenched position: "My mind is made up—you won't convince me otherwise." This used to be my attitude as a Trinitarian. I had my proof texts that I believed clearly taught God was a composite being and Jesus was part of the "Godhead." As far as I was concerned, it was what every knowledgeable Christian believed. Sure, I was aware that there were some who saw it differently, such as Arius and his followers back in the day. But in my mind, Christian orthodoxy had been established at the Council of Nicea in AD 325, and such heresies had well and truly been put to bed.

I now realize that I had only heard one side of the argument, and there was another side, which was far more coherent and compelling than I had ever imagined.

> In a lawsuit the first to speak seems right, until someone comes forward and cross-examines. (Prov. 18:17)

Solomon was right. If nobody questions what you've been told, you'll probably assume that what you've heard is the truth. It's never wise to come to a conclusion without hearing both sides of the story.

It's Too Hard

Others put the whole debate in the "too hard" category. They reason: "If theologians have been arguing and disagreeing about this for centuries, what hope have I got?" They despair at ever being able to figure it out. And they do have a point. Given that it's not clear cut, it can be confusing and a little daunting. Of course, those who throw their arms in the air and say "It's all too hard" may simply be expressing that they aren't that motivated or don't really care. But for those who are willing to explore, whatever your final conclusion may be, I'm sure you'll be enriched in the process.

> [Jesus] said to them, "Therefore every teacher of the law who has become a disciple in the kingdom of heaven is like the owner of a house who brings out of his storeroom new treasures as well as old." (Matt. 13:52)

There are some gems of understanding and insight to be gained as we ponder the Scriptures around this doctrine and consider what the Bible teaches about Jesus—including the very real possibility of "new treasure as well as old."

It's a Mystery

There are those who go beyond saying that the search is difficult. They say it's impossible. For them, God is incomprehensible: "… How unsearchable his judgments, and his paths beyond tracing out!" (Rom. 11:33). They conclude it's beyond our capacity to understand or figure God out, reasoning that it's one of those things we just won't be able to comprehend this side of Christ's return—because we "see only a reflection as in a mirror" (1 Cor. 13:12).

While I appreciate their point, it needs to be balanced by the fact that we have a God who is not silent—he has revealed himself to us, ultimately through his son (Heb. 1:1-2). Moreover, understanding God's revelation of himself is foundational to knowing him, having a meaningful relationship with him, and participating in his loving purposes for us and the world.

"Now this is eternal life: that they know you, the only true God, and Jesus Christ, whom you have sent" (John 17:3). God invites us to know him and grow in our understanding of him (2 Pet. 1:3-8). The Bible says:

> The secret things belong to the LORD our God, but the things revealed belong to us and to our children forever, that we may follow all the words of this law. (Deut. 29:29)

Before consigning God's nature and person to mystery and the unknowable, we should consider whether in fact we have fully received and understood what God has revealed to us about himself and about Jesus Christ whom he has sent.

It's Not Worth It

There are some who think that trying to understand the nature of God and interrelationship between Father, Son, and Spirit is all a bit esoteric. In the end, does it really matter? Will it make any practical difference in how I seek to live as a committed disciple of Jesus Christ? There are far more important issues to be concerned about, they think.

I can appreciate what they are saying. Would a cost-benefit analysis conducted on this theology recommend that it's worth investing time and effort? As mentioned above, there are some significant costs or liabilities to exploring this doctrine. Any possible benefit may hardly seem worthwhile in comparison. So once again the question: "Why bother?"

In chapter 6, several advantages for a Non-trinitarian view of Jesus are listed. However, at this point let me suggest three reasons why I believe it is important to examine this doctrine:[1]

---

1. Eric Miller, "5 Things You Lose When You Stop Believing Jesus is Almighty God," *Jehovah and Jesus*, April 14, 2021, https://bit.ly/3dBV6Xf.

The Truth Issue

Christians have a clear commitment to understand and live by the truth. In John chapter 8, Jesus teaches that the evil one is a deceiver—a liar from the beginning, in whom there is no truth (vv. 44-45). This is in contrast to the truth from the Father that Jesus has faithfully declared to his "sheep"—those who follow him and belong to him (vv. 28, 40, 45). Hence, his genuine disciples "hold to [his] teaching… [they] will know the truth and the truth will set [them] free" (vv. 31-32). Later, Jesus prays for his followers: "Sanctify them by the truth; your word is truth" (John 17:17). In seeking truth we are seeking God, his will and his ways, and a close relationship with him. And his truth will bring freedom, fullness of life, and Christian maturity.

In his epistle to his friend Gaius, John says, "I have no greater joy than to hear that my children are walking in the truth" (3 John 4). God does not lie (Titus 1:2) and is right and faithful in all he says and does (Pss. 33:4-5; 145:17). As his children, we have received his message of truth and have his Spirit of truth in us, and so are called to walk in his light, truth, and integrity (1 John 1:5-10).

For those who are in positions of teaching and leadership in the church, this is even more crucial. They need to "watch [their] life and doctrine closely" (1 Tim. 4:16). It's important not to "distort the word of God" (2 Cor. 4:2). They have an even greater responsibility to understand, live, and declare the truth of God's word "in God's household, which is the church of the living God, the pillar and foundation of the truth" (1 Tim. 3:15). So Paul exhorts Timothy: "Do your best to present yourself to God as one approved, a worker who does not need to be ashamed and who correctly handles the word of truth" (2 Tim. 2:15).

Therefore, if we love God and his word, have a yearning to know, understand, and live by his truth, and moreover if we want to correctly discern and present this truth to others, then our correct understanding of God and of Jesus is not something to dismiss lightly, or put in a basket labelled "too hard," "too controversial," "too costly," or whatever. It is worth some serious consideration and study.

For many years, a colleague and friend of mine, Reverend Graham Long, ran Wayside Chapel, a significant Christian mission and community service organization in King's Cross (the red-light district of downtown Sydney). Wayside Chapel ministers Christ's love to the homeless and destitute, the needy and vulnerable. Reverend Long has commented on more than one occasion that "we should worship Jesus less and follow him more." Although this statement is a little controversial, and probably deliberately provocative, I believe it has some validity.

It's not that we shouldn't give Jesus appropriate praise and honor, but in the Gospels Christ's call is to follow him (eg., Matt. 4:19; Mark 1:17; 2:14; Luke 9:59) in costly obedience and sacrificial service: "Whoever wants to be my disciple must deny themselves and take up their cross daily and follow me" (Luke 9:23). And in the epistles, while there is no command to worship Jesus, there is a repeated exhortation to follow and emulate him (eg., 1 Cor. 11:1; Eph. 4:13; Heb. 12:2; 1 Pet. 2:21; Rev. 14:4).

The doctrine of the Trinity can have the effect of diminishing Jesus' humanity and diluting his example, thereby dissipating his clarion call to devoted discipleship. Jesus is deified, mystified, etherealized, so that to once again quote Graham, "Christians care more about singing *to* him than living *for* him."

Thomas Jefferson, the third president of the United States, was a Non-trinitarian. He once stated: "When we shall have done away with the incomprehensible jargon of the Trinitarian arithmetic, that three are one, and one is three; when we shall have knocked down the artificial scaffolding reared to mask from view the simple structure of Jesus; when, in short, we shall have unlearned everything which has been taught since his day, and got back to the pure and simple doctrines he inculcated, we shall then be truly and worthily his disciples."[2]

---

2. Thomas Jefferson to Timothy Pickering, February 27, 1821, *Founders Online*, National Archives, https://founders.archives.gov/documents/Jefferson/98-01-02-1870.

It's a strong statement, but I believe he makes a valid point. To follow Jesus is to become more like him, to fashion our life on his, and align with him as our model. Therefore, it's important that we have a clear perception of who he is and how he lived. I'll have more to say about this in chapter 6, so I won't elaborate here beyond stating the general principle.

THE MISSIONAL ISSUE

Eric Chang was a highly educated and extremely successful evangelist and church leader. He had a heart to reach Muslims with the gospel, but found that the Christian doctrine of the Trinity was a significant barrier in appealing to Islamic adherents, who were fiercely monotheistic. His attempts to explain that the three persons of the Father, Son, and Spirit were only one God seemed less than convincing to them. It forced him back to re-examine what the Bible actually teaches on the subject. Like many others who have honestly considered what the Bible says (and doesn't say), he became convinced that a Trinitarian view was not scripturally supported. He subsequently wrote two books: *The Only True God* and *The Only Perfect Man*, listed in the Bibliography.

Whether or not you agree with his conclusion, the fact remains that the doctrine of the Trinity is a stumbling block in our evangelism to Jews and Muslims. In their strict monotheism they are skeptical about whether the Christian faith truly upholds one God as we claim it does. It is also confusing and logically problematic in our attempts to convince rationalistic non-believers of the credibility of our beliefs.

I am not suggesting that in our evangelism we should avoid difficult issues or genuine points of contention. Nor am I suggesting that, to make it more palatable, we water down what we believe. Rather, I argue that like the Apostle Paul, who became "all things to all people so that by all possible means [he] might save some" (1 Cor. 9:22), we remove all unnecessary barriers to non-believers receiving the gospel, especially if these barriers are unscriptural or non-essential.

For Chang, his motivation to explore the doctrine of the Trinity arose out of his missional heart, his desire to share the good news of Jesus in a way that was clear, uncluttered, and unhindered.

THE REAL ISSUE

While I acknowledge that there are many reasons people shy away from wanting to explore issues around the essential nature and relationship between the three members of the "Godhead," the biggest deterrent hasn't been mentioned yet. I believe it's more powerful than all the others combined, because it has to do with the heart rather than the head. It is much more an emotional, experiential, and relational issue than an intellectual or theological one.

Many Christians who have been schooled in Trinitarian doctrine believe it, not out of personal investigation and conviction, but because it has been the accepted belief of the church or wider faith community they belong to, or because it has been taught by people they respect and admire. To question it would seriously disrupt and undermine the credibility structures they have in place around their Christian faith. It would throw their world into an unthinkable upheaval.

Others have grown up seeing Jesus in a certain light, knowing him in a particular way, and relating to him in a certain manner. They have sung Trinitarian songs with gusto, worshipped him as God, prayed to him as equal to the Father, conceived of him in terms of "fully human, fully divine." To suggest otherwise is a bridge too far in terms of their Christian faith and personal experience. It would be like suggesting to somebody that the spouse they had been married to for 20 or 30 years is in some respects very different from how they have always understood them to be.

In hindsight, I believe the emotional and relational dimensions were what I struggled with most. It's why I took a lot more convincing than should have been needed before I was willing to honestly reconsider my position. I discern that same resistance in others when I discuss the topic with them. Often there comes a point where I sense it becomes too confronting for them. Their defenses engage and the walls come up. Paul observed that same response in the Jews he sought to engage with the gospel: a veil remained over their hearts and minds as they read the Old Testament Scriptures, preventing them from beholding the new revelation God had brought about in Christ (2 Cor. 3:14-16).

You may have experienced that barrier in people who close their hearts to the gospel when they begin to realize the fundamental change it will make if they believe and accept it. As Christians, we hope they will remain open, because although it does involve uncertainty, change, and even personal cost, in the end the gospel is more than worth it. I believe the same applies in our present discussion.

> And no one pours new wine into old wineskins. Otherwise, the new wine will burst the skins; the wine will run out and the wineskins will be ruined. No, new wine must be poured into new wineskins. And no one after drinking old wine wants the new, for they say, "The old is better." (Luke 5:37-39)

In Greek, the last word here is *chrestos* which means "good, pleasant, serviceable, agreeable." The one who is used to drinking old wine is content with it, and is unlikely to seek or prefer something new. Jesus' remarks here are addressed to the scribes and Pharisees, who were not open to his new message. The old traditions and teachings they were accustomed to had been serving their purposes well, and they weren't about to change.

This leads me to the question: Have you come to your present position, be it Trinitarian or Non-trinitarian, as the result of thorough research and careful consideration? Have you looked at both sides of the biblical and historical evidence in a fair and reasonable manner and arrived at a conclusion which you humbly and prayerfully believe is the truth? Or is your belief simply the one you know, are used to, or are comfortable with?

Many Christians have come to their position solely from what they have been told: what's orthodox, acceptable, and serviceable. Or it's what they prefer, finding it agreeable because theologically, emotionally, or relationally it is what they're comfortable with. They aren't open to taste "new wine" or examine anything different. I don't seek to criticize; I'm simply stating the reality of the situation. That's exactly where I was for many years.

In Acts 17:22-34, when Paul presented the good news about Jesus at the Areopagus in Athens, we read of three distinct responses from the crowd. Some sneered. They were unconvinced and rejected the message. Some believed. They were convinced and became followers. Some "want[ed] to hear [Paul] again on this subject" (v. 32). They were not yet convinced, but open to explore further.

Whichever of these three responses may be your position after reading this book, my prayer is that you will maintain the attitude of the Berean Jews that we read about just prior to Paul's sojourn in Athens. Paul's teaching on the Scriptures was certainly new and radically different to anything they had encountered before, but they were judged of "noble character... for they received the message with great eagerness and examined the Scriptures every day to see if what Paul said was true" (Acts 17:11).

Similarly, my prayer is that you would be willing to consider what is presented...

Openly. With humility and a teachable spirit.

Expectantly. Our search should be undertaken courageously, not anxiously. Ultimately, God's truth leads to freedom and life.

Biblically. I believe that the Scriptures are the divinely inspired and trustworthy revelation of God (2 Tim. 3:16; 2 Pet. 1:21) and should be used as our ultimate and authoritative guide in all matters of life and faith. Let's be willing to place our views and opinions in submission to God's truth as revealed in the Bible.

> "For my thoughts are not your thoughts, neither are your ways my ways," declares the LORD. "As the heavens are higher than the earth, so are my ways higher than your ways and my thoughts than your thoughts." (Isa. 55:8)

May God grant us all wisdom and grace as we humbly, openly, and courageously seek the truth about his son, our glorious Lord and Savior Jesus.

Summary:

While there are reasons some may not wish to re-examine their Christology outside a Trinitarian paradigm, there are also some good reasons why I believe we should. It's because we love God's word and are committed to seeking his truth. It's because our devotion to Jesus calls us to know him truly and make him known clearly, as the Scriptures reveal him to be. In the words of a prayer attributed to Saint Richard of Chichester (1197-1253), our heart for our Lord Jesus is "to know him more clearly, love him more dearly, follow him more nearly—day by day."

This book is for those with the desire to know, the curiosity to explore, the courage to change, the integrity of a humble and teachable spirit.

CHAPTER 3

WHY QUESTION?

MANY PEOPLE CONSIDER THE doctrine of the Trinity to be set in stone. The purpose of this chapter is to begin to challenge this assumption. Maybe this doctrine is more questionable than many realize. The history behind it, the processes which gave rise to it, the scriptural support for it, and the rationality within it, are unconvincing to say the least. It contains a number of inherent contradictions that can't be satisfactorily resolved by reason or biblical input.

There are three key facts[1] that most Christians are unaware of when it comes to the theological construct of the Trinity:

1. It was a Post-Apostolic Development

The following is a small sample of quotes written by Trinitarian scholars:

> It must be admitted by everyone who has the rudiments of an historical sense that the doctrine of the Trinity formed no part of the original message. St. Paul did not know it, and would have been unable to understand the meaning of the terms used in the theological formula on which the Church ultimately agreed.[2] No responsible NT scholar would claim that the doctrine of the Trinity was taught by Jesus or preached by the earliest Christians or consciously held by any writer of the NT. It was in fact slowly worked out in

---

1. By calling them "facts," I don't mean that they have not been contested, but rather that they are well established by fair-minded historians and theologians.

2. W. R. Matthews, *God in Christian Experience* (London: James Nisbet and Co., 1930), 180.

the course of the first few centuries in an attempt to give an intelligible doctrine of God.[3]

...the developed concept of three coequal partners in the Godhead found in later creedal formulations cannot be clearly detected within the confines of the canon.[4]

Indeed throughout the New Testament while there is belief in God the Father, in Jesus the Son and in God's Holy Spirit, there is no doctrine of one God in three persons (modes of being), no doctrine of a "triune God," a "Trinity."[5]

As you can see, many Trinitarians admit that the doctrine itself is not specifically or explicitly taught in the Bible. However, they generally maintain that the seeds of this doctrine—its underlying concepts— are expressed therein. It was the theological trajectory these New Testament writers were embarking on, they argue, even if the doctrine wasn't fully formed until later.

Let's put aside for the moment what the New Testament authors may have believed and expressed in their writings (which we'll consider in chapter 5) and ask what the historical evidence indicates: the controversies of the early church, the formal creedal statements, and the writings of the apostolic and early church fathers.

New Testament Controversies

He said to them, "How foolish you are, and how slow to believe all that the prophets have spoken! Did not the Messiah have to suffer these things and then enter his glory?" And beginning with Moses and all the Prophets, he explained to them what was said in all the Scriptures concerning himself. (Luke 24:25-27)

The significant controversies about the Messiah that were strongly

---

3. A. T. Hanson, *The Image of the Invisible God* (London: SCM Press, 1982), 87.

4. Bruce M. Metzger and Michael D. Coogan, eds., *Oxford Companion to the Bible* (Oxford: Oxford University Press, 1993), 782.

5. Hans Küng, *Christianity: Its Essence and History* (London: SCM Press, 1995), 95.

contested in the New Testament were: his death by crucifixion, his resurrection, and his subsequent ascension and glorification.

It's no wonder that these three facts were hotly debated. They didn't align with Jewish expectations of the Anointed One. The Jews anticipated the Messiah as an all-conquering king, the ultimate ruler of God's kingdom on earth, not a suffering servant executed in humiliation as a criminal. Hence the cross was "a stumbling block to [the] Jews" (1 Cor. 1:23).

The bodily resurrection of the Messiah was also unexpected, as the Jews believed in only one resurrection, which was of those in Sheol on the Day of the Lord—a day of judgment for everyone who had ever lived and reward for the faithful. That's why, along with the cross, the fact of Jesus resurrection was "of first importance" (1 Cor. 15:3-4).

Likewise, Jesus' failure to defeat Israel's enemies, the Romans, and usher in the kingdom of God at that time was a problem to the Jews—then and since. The disciples questioned Jesus just prior to his being caught up from them in the clouds: "Lord, are you at this time going to restore the kingdom to Israel?" (Acts 1:6). This was a perfectly legitimate question given some of the Old Testament prophecies about the Messiah, but certain details concerning his ascension, glorification, and future second coming were not fully understood.

As you read through the book of Acts you will discover that these are the three facts that the apostles continue to preach and debate, especially with the Jews (Acts 2:22-36; 3:17-26; 5:29-32; 10:34-43; 13:26-41; 17:2-4; 17:29-31; 26:19-23). You'll also notice that several times they assert that they were saying nothing beyond what the prophets and Moses said would happen (Acts 26:25; 28:23; 3:24; 10:43; 13:33). Even though some Jewish expectations at the time about the Messiah had not been fulfilled in Jesus, the events that had unfolded were all predicted within the prophecies of the Old Testament. They confirmed Jesus was indeed God's promised Anointed One, the one the nation had been waiting for.

These basic Christological tenets differed from previous perceptions, so they were strongly proclaimed and debated from the inception of the church on the Day of Pentecost (Acts 2:14-36). If the Jewish understanding regarding the Messiah's identity and essence did not conform to the truth, if it needed significant redefining, why is there no attempt to directly address this issue in the New Testament?

Nowhere is there reference to a debate over Jesus being "fully human and fully God," or being himself God or on the same level as God. It doesn't appear at all on the landscape of first-century church history, whereas it looms large, at center stage in the church history of the fourth and fifth centuries.

This silence is remarkable because the early church was strongly Jewish and the Jews were strongly monotheistic. Any suggestion that Jesus was *Yahweh*, or a part of *Yahweh*, or even equal to *Yahweh*, would have been vehemently resisted, would it not? This silence is certainly difficult to explain if, as claimed by some, Trinitarian doctrine existed from the outset, from the earliest days of the church.[6]

CREEDS

Many creedal statements were written and reformulated by various church leaders, groups, and councils in the early centuries of the church. Below are some of those most widely accepted and commonly known. As you read through, notice the evolution:

- From basic, simple statements, to more complicated and convoluted phraseology.
- From foundational biblical facts to greater interpretation and metaphysical analysis.
- From scriptural words and language to philosophical terms and expressions.
- From Non-trinitarian (or neutral) theology to Trinitarian theology.

---

6. For other absences in the New Testament that seem inexplicable if the authors were Trinitarian or had a deity Christology, see "Podcast 191 – Ware's Outline of the Testimony of Scripture Against the Trinity," by Dale Tuggy, *Trinities,* July 17, 2017, https://trinities.org/blog/podcast-191-wares-outline-of-the-testimony-of-scripture-against-the-trinity/; and also "Podcast 189 – The unfinished business of the Reformation," by Dale Tuggy, *Trinities,* July 3, 2017, https://trinities.org/blog/podcast-189-the-unfinished-business-of-the-reformation/.

The Old Roman Creed[7]

ca. AD 150

I believe in God the Father Almighty;
And in Christ Jesus His only Son our Lord;
Who was born of the Holy Spirit and the virgin Mary; Crucified under Pontius Pilate and buried; The third day he rose from the dead;
He ascended into heaven; He sits at the right hand of the Father; Thence he shall come to judge the living and the dead;
And in the Holy Spirit, the holy Church,
The remission of sins, the resurrection of the flesh.

Apostles' Creed[8]

Second Century AD[9]

I believe in God the Father Almighty, invisible and impassible. And in Jesus Christ, His only Son, our Lord; Who was born from the Holy Ghost, of the Virgin Mary; Was crucified under Pontius Pilate, and buried; He descended to hell; on the third day he rose again from the dead. He ascended to the heavens; he sitteth at the right hand of the Father; Thence he is to come to judge the quick and the dead. And in the Holy Ghost; The remission of sins. The resurrection of this flesh.

Nicene / Constantinopolitan Creed[10]

AD 325 / 381

We believe in one God, the Father Almighty, maker of heaven and earth and of all things visible and invisible. And in one Lord Jesus Christ, the only begotten Son of God, begotten of his Father before all worlds, Light of Light, very God of very God, begotten not made, being of one substance with the Father, by whom all things

---

7. Justo L. González, *The Story of Christianity* (Peabody, MA: Hendrickson Publishers, 2001), 63.

8. Tyrannius Rufinus, *A Commentary on the Apostles' Creed*, trans. William H. Fremantle, Nicene and Post-Nicene Fathers: 2nd series, vol. 3, eds. Philip Schaff and Henry Wace (1892; repr., Peabody, MA: Hendrickson Publishers, 1999), 541-542.

9. Although this creed was not fully developed until ca. AD 700, it is similar to the "Rule of Faith" written by some of the early church fathers.

10. Henry R. Percival, ed. and trans., *The Seven Ecumenical Councils*, Nicene and Post-Nicene Fathers: 2nd series, vol. 14, eds. Philip Schaff and Henry Wace (1900; repr., Peabody, MA: Hendrickson Publishers, 2004), 163.

were made. Who for us men and for our salvation came down from heaven and was incarnate by the Holy Ghost and the Virgin Mary, and was made man, and was crucified also for us under Pontius Pilate. He suffered and was buried, and the third day he rose again according to the Scriptures, and ascended into heaven, and sitteth at the Right Hand of the Father. And he shall come again with glory to judge both the quick and the dead. Whose kingdom shall have no end.

And [we believe] in the Holy Ghost, the Lord and Giver-of-Life, who proceedeth from the Father, who with the Father and the Son together is worshipped and glorified, who spake by the prophets. And [we believe] in one, holy, Catholic and Apostolic Church. We acknowledge one Baptism for the remission of sins, [and] we look for the resurrection of the dead and the life of the world to come. Amen.

Chalcedonian Creed[11]
AD 451 (Extract)

...[O]ur Lord Jesus Christ is to be confessed as one and the same [Person], that he is perfect in Godhead and perfect in manhood, very God and very man, of a reasonable soul and [human] body consisting, consubstantial with the Father as touching his Godhead, and consubstantial with us as touching his manhood; made in all things like unto us, sin only excepted; begotten of his Father before the worlds according to his Godhead; but in these last days for us men and for our salvation born [into the world] of the Virgin Mary, the Mother of God according to his manhood. This one and the same Jesus Christ, the only-begotten Son [of God] must be confessed to be in two natures, unconfusedly, immutably, indivisibly, inseparably [united], and that without the distinction of natures being taken away by such union, but rather the peculiar property of each nature being preserved and being united in one Person and subsistence, not separated or divided into two persons, but one and the same Son and only-begotten, God the Word, our Lord Jesus Christ...

Later creeds, such as the Athanasian Creed (ca. AD 500) continued this trend in Trinitarian theological speculation even further, stating that anyone not in agreement would "perish eternally."

As revealed in these accepted church creeds, Trinitarian theology was not present in the earlier statements of faith, but only in those that were formulated later—in the fourth and fifth centuries. Historically, they support a subsequent Trinitarian construct, developed much later than the New Testament.

---

11. ibid., 264-265.

EARLY WRITINGS: CHURCH FATHERS

Trinitarians often use quotes from the apostolic and early church fathers to bolster the perception that Trinitarian theology was already developed and generally accepted soon after the New Testament had been written. These church fathers include Ignatius (AD 50-117), Polycarp (AD 70-155), Justin Martyr (AD 100-165), Iraneus (AD 115-190), Tertullian (AD 160-215), and Origen (AD 184-253).

At face value, the quotations Trinitarians frequently select create the impression that the church fathers were generally of a Trinitarian persuasion. But this seriously misrepresents their doctrinal beliefs and theological positions for the following reasons:

- The quotations used by Trinitarian writers are cherry-picked and not truly representative. Many other statements from these same authors, which create a very different impression or express contrary doctrine, are ignored.
- Usually they are quoted out of context,[12] be it the immediate text or the wider reading of the author's works, which give a fuller and different understanding of their position. For example, Origen was quoted by both pro-Nicene and anti-Nicene factions to support their competing positions.
- The historical context is also important in their terminology and nomenclature. As Paul comments, in the Roman empire there were "many 'gods' and many 'lords'" (1 Cor. 8:5).
  At the time, such terms were not used with uniformity by all authors. Similarly, the word "trinity," which came into use in the third century, only gradually evolved to its eventual theological meaning.
- As today, not all these early church leaders and authors were aligned. There was considerable disagreement and debate

---

12. For some examples of this, see "Did Christians Believe in the Trinity before the Council of Nicaea in 325?" by Sean Finnegan, *Restitutio*, April 20, 2019, https://restitutio.org/2019/04/20/did-christians-believe-in-the-trinity-before-the-council-of-nicaea-in-325/.

between them on many points of doctrine. In reality, there was a very disparate theology generally, and Christology specifically, among the apostolic and early church fathers.

- When the Roman Emperor Theodosius officially banned all Non-trinitarian Christianity in AD 381, many of the patristic, non-compliant documents were destroyed, while Trinitarian documents survived. Also, certain documents from the church fathers were subsequently changed or redacted to comply with the orthodox position. For example, in AD 397, Rufinus, a devotee of Origen, wanting to exonerate the reputation of his master, simply removed anything Christologically "questionable" from Origen's writings.

Of course, the bottom line is that these writings are not inspired in the same way, or with the same level of authority, as the Scriptures.

Patristics (the study of the writings and beliefs of the early church fathers) is a very demanding discipline. The best scenario would be for a team of fair-minded researchers to systematically and objectively wade through all the relevant Christian literature prior to AD 381 to see who believed what and discern the overall framework of theology in the period.

This would be a much more honest and scholarly approach than simply cherry-picking and proof-texting certain statements, out of context, that support what you want them to prove. Until now, probably the most comprehensive investigation to date on Christological and Trinitarian belief in these writings has been undertaken by Alvan Lamson. His earth-shattering conclusion is as follows:

> After what has been said in the foregoing [395 pages] we are prepared to re-assert, in conclusion, that the modern doctrine of the Trinity is not found in any document or relic belonging to the Church of the first three centuries. Letters, art, usage, theology, worship, creed, hymn, chant, doxology, ascription, commemorative rite, and festive observance,

so far as any remains or any record of them are preserved, coming down from early times, are, as regards this doctrine, an absolute blank. They testify, so far as they testify at all, to the supremacy of the Father, the only true God; and to the inferior and derived nature of the Son. There is nowhere among these remains a co-equal Trinity. The cross is there; Christ is there as the Good Shepherd, the Father's hand placing a crown, or victor's wreath, on his head; but no undivided Three—co-equal, infinite, self-existent, and eternal. This was a conception to which the age had not arrived. It was of later origin.[13]

2. The Process For Its Acceptance As Orthodox Was Flawed

"Fake news" is a term that has gained currency in recent times. It refers to news reports that are not accurate, either because they are very selective in what they choose to report on (or conveniently overlook) or because of the very biased way in which facts are presented. What is fed to the general population is an interpretation of events, even though the reality may be very different.

We could also coin the term "fake history," because the above tendencies are only exaggerated over time. As the actual eyewitnesses and succeeding generations pass away, accountability of reporting diminishes and facts become more difficult to verify. Added to that is the dynamic that the winners write history. Hence, the official record tends to be a one-sided interpretation and perspective.

I remember being told in theological college that when Christianity became an accepted religion in the Roman Empire under Constantine, there was a need to redress some heresies that were around at the time. Some variant Christological views had arisen, in particular the Arian controversy. However, I was told, these were all resolved at the Council of Nicea in AD 325.

---

13. Alvan Lamson, *The Church of the First Three Centuries,* 2nd ed. (Boston: Walker, Fuller, and Co., 1865), 39.

Orthodoxy was established and the controversy put to bed.

I now realize that this was "fake history." The reality of what actually happened differs considerably. Let me mention a few details that aren't widely known which present another narrative and perspective:

Prior to AD 325, the theological landscape in Christian churches across the Roman Empire was diverse, confused, and in flux. The scriptural canon had yet to be established. Controversies, false doctrines, and variant theologies abounded.

This is reflected not only in the documents of the church fathers and writings of the pagan philosopher Celsus during the second century, but has now been significantly confirmed through the discovery in Egypt, in 1945, of the Nag Hammadi documents.

Within this disparate ecclesiological and theological mix, one fact is generally agreed on by historians: prior to Nicea, a subordinationist Christology was the majority view—the orthodox position. Subordinationism is the belief that Christ is not on the same level as his heavenly Father, but in some way (or ways) subordinate to him and under him.

Nicea was the first grand council. It was hosted by the emperor Constantine and sponsored by the state. The church leaders (bishops) who attended received a level of acceptance, favor, power, and luxury that was previously unimagined. The reported number of those who attended differ in the accounts, but it was probably close to 300, representing only about one sixth of all bishops in the empire at the time.

Although sympathetic to the Christian faith, Constantine retained his pagan beliefs and practices. He wasn't even baptized until just before his death. Prior to Nicea, Bishop Hosius of Cordova was somewhat of a personal advisor to Constantine. In preparation for the council, Hosius was commissioned to undertake an investigation and make recommendations on the controversy that existed between Arius (who saw Jesus as the son of God) and Athanasius (who believed Jesus was also God the Son). Among other things,

Hosius recommended that:[14]

- Compromise was not possible (perhaps reflecting Greek logic and categorical, "either-or" thinking then in vogue).
- Arianism would reduce the role or influence of the institutional church and needed to be repressed.
- Athanasius' views would better serve the interests of the empire.
- A strategy needed to be employed to end the division quickly and decisively.

Hence, an anti-Arian statement of faith was drafted (complete with a list of "anathemas" attached) and promulgated prior to the meeting of the council. With Constantine as the host and Hosius as the presiding officer at Nicea, considerable pressure was applied for all to comply. Many of the bishops signed the statement under duress. Their supposed endorsement notwithstanding, bitter disagreement and strong debate continued. Also of note is that the Holy Spirit did not feature significantly in the deliberations at Nicea; it was not officially included as part of the Christian deity until some 50 years later.

One point of considerable contention was the introduction of philosophical terms such as "*ousia*" and "*hypostasis*" into the discussion. These words were susceptible to many shades of meaning relating to substance, reality, being, type, essence, person. Those nuances would be the subject of confusion, controversy, and debate in this and consequent councils.

The intent in introducing these philosophical terms was to force the Arians (or their position) out of the church. But in so doing, the winners at Nicea were admitting that Scripture alone was inadequate to settle disputes and that the Bible doesn't fully explain or define certain matters that we need to know. They were no longer "explaining spiritual realities with Spirit-taught words" (1 Cor. 2:13).

The Council of Nicea did not bring about the theological

---

14. Richard E. Rubenstein, *When Jesus became God: The Struggle to Define Christianity during the Last Days of Rome* (New York: Harcourt Brace & Co., 1999), 44, 91-92.

unity it hoped to achieve. The relationship between Father and Son became an ongoing theological battleground, which virtually split the church ever more violently over the ensuing 50 years. Within three years of Nicea, most of its decisions had been overturned and the excommunicated Arians had been reinstated.

In fact, church councils were convened almost every year after Nicea, with their determinations invariably wavering between pro- and anti-Nicene theology.[15] The determinations and statements of faith accepted by one council were generally ruled unacceptable and repudiated by the next. As a result, Athanasius was condemned and excommunicated as a heretic on at least five separate occasions, with Arius suffering a similar fate.

A number of these councils were larger and more ecumenical than the Council of Nicea. For example, the Council of Rumini-Selucia in AD 359, which adopted an Arian creed, had over 500 bishops in attendance, with a fair representation of both Latin-speaking bishops from the West and Greek-speaking bishops from the East. However, because its determinations were eventually outlawed as unorthodox, the records of such councils have virtually disappeared from official church history.

Arius died suddenly during the Council of Constantine in AD 336—his followers suspected he had been poisoned. But his theology persisted as a major faction within Christendom for the next 40 years. Athanasius died in AD 373. About that time the Cappadocian Fathers developed a theology of the Holy Spirit as a separate person within the "Godhead." Then, in AD 380, Emperor Theodosius outlawed Arianism in a hard-line approach to unify the church and empire. Possessing Arian views or literature became a crime punishable by the state. These developments led to a version of the Trinity immortalized in the Nicene Creed, ratified at the Council of Constantinople in AD 381. Thereafter, it was considered official.

The truth is that the controversy over the nature and person

---

15. R. P. C. Hanson, *The Search for the Christian Doctrine of God* (Grand Rapids, MI: Baker Academic, 2005) ch. 7-19.

of Jesus was not settled at the Council of Nicea. It continued to evolve and to be debated for the next several decades. The process was convoluted, with theological considerations being highly influenced by machinations within both state and ecclesiastical powers at the time. Eventually it was resolved more politically than scripturally.

In reality, Trinitarian theology developed some considerable time after the New Testament writings. It was a hotly-debated, gradual evolution, fraught with controversy, disagreement, political interference, and ecclesiastical intrigue. The process was very flawed. I hasten to add that this does not, in itself, necessarily mean that the outcome is therefore wrong. But it should alert us to two possible errors:

FIRST—ACCEPTING DETERMINATIONS OF CHURCH COUNCILS AS DOCTRINALLY INFALLIBLE (OR EVEN AUTHORITATIVE). We have seen how contradictory they were. Protestants have always chosen which of the early council decisions they would accept anyway. For example, we don't accept the exaltation and veneration of Mary, the doctrine of the immaculate conception, praying to the saints as intermediaries, and so forth.

SECOND—ASSUMING THE NEW TESTAMENT AUTHORS WROTE FROM A TRINITARIAN PARADIGM. In fact, unless they explicitly enunciate or teach to the contrary, we should assume they are not writing from that perspective. To read a theological construct that came into being subsequently back into their statements is to compromise the integrity of their writings.

3. It Contains Inherent Rational And Theological Discrepancies

As we've seen, both before and after the Council of Nicea the doctrinal bone of contention that divided the church was about the person and nature of Jesus. Was Jesus fully God or not? Was he the Son of God or God the Son? Was he under God or a part of God? The eventual outcome was that those who believed Jesus was fully God prevailed, and the doctrine of the Trinity became mandatory for all Christians to believe. Jesus was considered to be co-eternal, co-equal, and co-essential with the Father.

However, this Trinitarian theological construct has some inherent scriptural or logical inconsistencies and contradictions which cannot be easily ignored:

- The Judeo-Christian faith is thoroughly and ardently monotheistic. Jesus himself affirmed its foundational statement of faith, recited daily by the Jews: "Hear, O Israel: the LORD our God, the LORD is one" (Deut. 6:4; Mark 12:29). How can you have a singular God who is also plural? How can you explain three "persons", who constitute one "being"?

- How can Jesus be both "fully human" and "fully God"? How can you combine that which is inherently limited with that which is intrinsically unlimited? What is the interplay between these two natures, and how does such a composite person operate?

- How can Jesus be eternal, yet begotten by God? "Begotten" contradicts any notion of an uncreated, eternal being. Trinitarians try to address this conundrum by speaking of him being "eternally begotten." But not only is this an oxymoron, it runs counter to the scriptural witness, which speaks of Jesus being begotten at a point in time: "You are my Son, *today* I have become your father" (Ps. 2:7; Heb. 1:5; emphasis added).

- The Bible says that "God cannot be tempted" (James 1:13), but Jesus was tempted (Matt. 11:1-4)—in fact, he was tempted "in every way, just as we are" (Heb. 4:15). Some Trinitarians even assert that Jesus' sinlessness is proof that he must have been God. But if that is the case, how can he have been completed or "made perfect" through his resisting temptation (Heb. 5:9; 7:19)? And how can he be an example for us to follow in obedience and Christian living (1 Pet. 2:21; 1 John 4:17)?

- We know that God "alone is immortal" and therefore unable to die (1 Tim. 6:16; see also Rom. 1:23), yet Jesus was killed. And "God...brought back from the dead our Lord Jesus" (Heb. 13:20).
- We read that "no one has seen or can see" God (1 Tim. 6:16), and that "no one has ever seen God" (John 1:18; 1 John 4:12), yet Jesus was seen.
- God "knows everything" (1 John 3:20), yet Jesus himself admitted that he didn't have complete knowledge, and that there were things that his Father knew that he himself did not (Matt. 24:36; Mark 13:32).
- Why would "all authority in heaven and on earth" have to be *given* to Jesus (Matt. 28:18)? Wouldn't this already be his by virtue of him being God?
- If Jesus is God, how can he have a God over him (Rom. 15:6; 1 Cor. 11:3; 15:28; Eph. 1:3, 17; Rev. 1:6; 3:12)?

Trinitarians are very much aware of these problems, and have sought to address and explain them in various ways—often with analogies and arguments that are more philosophical than biblical. I won't examine those arguments in terms of how convincing or otherwise they may be, but it should be noted that, these arguments notwithstanding, Trinitarians themselves often struggle to deal with the seemingly irreconcilable contradictions inherent within their paradigm, and therefore appeal to "mystery." When hard pressed to explain the inexplicable or understand the non-sensical, this is seemingly their default position.

They declare that as finite human beings with limited intellectual capacity, we cannot hope to comprehend an infinite God beyond our understanding. But this claim is something of a *non sequitur*. The issue is not trying to comprehend the incomprehensible God, but rather understanding and making sense of what he has clearly made known about himself:

> The secret things belong to the LORD our God, but the things revealed belong to us and to our children forever, that we may follow all the words of this law. (Deut. 29:29)

Delving into the "secret things" and hidden knowledge was the domain of Gnosticism. But it is not the "secret things," which he has kept hidden, that we are trying to discern. Rather, we are seeking to understand the "things revealed," which he has given to us for our understanding and obedience, for communication and teaching the next generation. These two are not to be confused.

The problem is that Trinitarians use the word "mystery" (Greek: *musterion*) in a Gnostic sense, or at least in a very different sense, than is generally used in the New Testament:

> I do not want you to be ignorant of this mystery... (Rom. 11:25)

> ...the revelation of the mystery hidden for long ages past, but now revealed and made known through the prophetic writings by the command of the eternal God... (Rom. 16:25-26)

> No, we declare God's wisdom, a mystery that has been hidden... (1 Cor. 2:7)

> ...entrusted with the mysteries God has revealed. (1 Cor. 4:1)

> He made known to us the mystery of his will... (Eph. 1:9)

> ...the mystery made known to me by revelation... (Eph. 3:3)

> ...the mystery of Christ...has now been revealed by the Spirit to God's holy apostles and prophets. (Eph. 3:4-5)

> ...so that I will fearlessly make known the mystery of the gospel. (Eph. 6:19)

> ...the mystery that has been kept hidden...but is now disclosed to the Lord's people. (Col. 1:26)

...so that they may have the full riches of complete understanding, in order that they may know the mystery of God... (Col. 2:2)

...so that we may proclaim the mystery of Christ... (Col. 4:3)

In virtually every case where the word mystery is used, it does not refer to some unfathomable or esoteric truth beyond our comprehension. Rather, it refers to *information that was previously hidden but has now been revealed by God* and can be clearly understood, explained, and communicated to others.

While our understanding is incomplete, and we do not yet "know fully, even as [we] are fully known" (1 Cor. 13:12), that doesn't stop us from knowing the many things God has revealed about himself, his will and ways. It doesn't stop us from thinking about him intelligently, rationally, and reasonably. "Mystery" can't be used as a cop-out or cover-up for what defies good sense or exegesis.

We have already noted the absence of any controversy within the New Testament that would have obviously ensued if the apostles believed or proclaimed that Jesus was equal to, or a part of, *Yahweh*. A further significant point to make is that the contradictions inherent within the Trinitarian paradigm (such as listed above) are never acknowledged nor addressed by any New Testament author. This too is quite remarkable.

Imagine the enormous challenges that Christianity presented to the Jewish faith as traditionally understood and practiced in the first century. There were many controversies over issues like:

- law verses grace as the basis for acceptance by God (Rom. 1:16-17; 3:21-28; 5:1-2; Gal. 3)
- whether believers were bound by the law of Moses and needed to be circumcised (Rom. 2:25-27; 4:9-12; Gal. 2:1-5; 5:2)
- the keeping of the Sabbath and holy days (Rom. 14:5)
- meat sacrificed to idols (Rom. 14; 1 Cor. 8; Acts 15)
- marriage and divorce (1 Cor. 7)
- how the resurrection would work when Jesus returned

(1 Cor. 15:12-57; 2 Cor. 5:1-10; 2 Thess. 2:1-12).

Paul and others did not hesitate to address such questions and issues. They didn't shy away from controversies and potential points of friction.

But we see no attempt whatsoever to acknowledge or address any of the dilemmas that would have been inherent within a Trinitarian understanding, if it had existed. How can Jesus be at the same time fully human and fully God, have a God yet be God, begotten yet uncreated, perfect yet needing to be perfected, truly God yet limited, tempted, killed?

Of all the conflicts between Christianity and traditional Judaism, this would have been the biggest of all, overshadowing everything else by far. Any attempt to dismantle or redefine strict monotheism would have been bitterly fought by the Jewish believers. Yet there is no mention of such a controversy anywhere, nor is there any attempt to address the conflict this would have necessarily presented.

I have yet to hear any reasonable or satisfactory explanation for this notable silence of discussion in the New Testament on Trinitarian doctrine, or on the dilemmas surrounding it, other than the obvious one: it was not under consideration at the time.

If all Trinitarians were to admit that their theological construct was a later development, subsequent to the New Testament writings, then this silence would be understandable. But many advocate that Trinitarian doctrine was inherent within the Christian faith from the very inception of the church, and that the Gospel writers and apostles bear witness to it.

Trinitarian theology and its inherent dilemmas don't seem to be anywhere on the radar of the New Testament writers, however. Rather, they seem to be problems of the construct's own making, only introduced and addressed centuries later. The challenge for Trinitarians is that they have a paradigm that is not only unintelligible, but unexplained in the Bible—at least in any way that is specific or instructive.

Summary:

Many people consider the doctrine of the Trinity as irrefutable and unquestionable. It is orthodox across mainstream Christendom; seemingly everyone believes it, the knowledgeable and theologically trained subscribe to it.

However, there is a growing chorus of biblical scholars and Christian believers who dare to differ. The historical evidence points strongly to its development subsequent to the New Testament writings, with its promotion and ultimate dominance resulting from a flawed process.

The doctrine contains a number of inherent inconsistencies and contradictions that cannot be satisfactorily resolved by reason or direct biblical teaching. God is not the author of confusion, so maybe an open-minded re-examination is in order.

CHAPTER 4

WHAT WENT WRONG?

I CONTEND THAT THE EVOLUTION of Trinitarian theology was not a natural development arising out of scriptural teaching, but a departure from it. I am not alone in this—a significant and growing number of biblical scholars hold this view.

If that is indeed the case, it raises the question: how did the church leaders and theologians of the fourth century get it so wrong? And if they did go off the rails, why wasn't it subsequently corrected? I believe the answers to those questions are not only insightful, but essential to us addressing any flawed exegesis around Trinitarian Christology today. Otherwise, we are in danger of repeating the same errors they did.

1. Cultural Shift

Hellenization, the spread of Greek culture and thinking, was pervasive, especially in the Eastern Roman Empire before and after the time of Christ. The Jews were mostly successful in their resistance to its influence because of their strong scriptural and cultural foundations. They saw Greek rationalistic and philosophical thinking as "gentile" and "worldly" and therefore to be rejected. However, when the gospel began to spread beyond Judea, and as the number of gentile converts increased, the infiltration of Greek thinking became a very real threat to the early church.

Paul warned against such philosophical incursions:

> See to it that no one takes you captive through hollow and
> deceptive philosophy, which depends on human tradition
> and the elemental spiritual forces of this world rather than

on Christ. (Col. 2:8)

Likewise, Peter warned Christians "scattered throughout the provinces" of Rome:

> But there were also false prophets among the people, just as there will be false teachers among you. They will secretly introduce destructive heresies, even denying the sovereign Lord who bought them—bringing swift destruction on themselves. (2 Pet. 2:1)

Many scholars believe that John's epistles were written to address some of the Gnostic concepts that had already begun to take hold in certain Christian communities.

What we need to appreciate is that to accurately understand the Bible, it should be read in its historical and cultural context. The Greeks believed in many gods, whereas the Jews were adamantly, ardently monotheistic (Deut. 6:4). The Greeks were familiar with composite natures within their "demigods," who were both human and divine, whereas the Hebrews did not have such a concept (Num. 23:19). The Greeks considered the human soul or spirit to be something preexistent, ongoing and independent from the individual—a Platonic separation from the body. But this was foreign to the more holistic understanding of the Hebrews (Gen. 2:7).

Thus, the theological concept of the Trinity could be accommodated comfortably with a classic Greek worldview, whereas it would not ever have been contemplated within a classic Hebrew one.

As we read and interpret the Bible, there is a sense in which we need to think like an ancient Middle Easterner (Hebrew), not like a modern Westerner, though much of our intellectual heritage stems from classical Greek perceptions. The principles of Greek logic and philosophy that were foundational to much of the theological reflection behind the fourth- and fifth-century councils and creeds are written on a different set of assumptions from the Hebrew Scriptures. The Greek mindset of intellectual analysis, metaphysical reflection, and conceptual abstraction were all quite foreign to the Hebrew ethos and Scriptures, not to mention such terms as *"ousia," "hypostasis,"* "unbegotten," "consubstantial," and so forth.

Exacerbating this intellectual drift were certain prejudices of the time. Theologians and church leaders became quite enamored with Greek philosophical and metaphysical contemplation. Churches of Christ scholar Robert Hach observes:

> The story of how Greek philosophy, with its synthesis of rationalism and mysticism...penetrated and permeated the Christian tradition, forever altering Christian faith, is virtually an open secret insofar as it oozes out the pores of the literature of church history and theology. The open secret continues to be kept, no doubt, due to its staggering implications.[1]

On the other hand, Jewish Christian believers became increasingly marginalized. The Palestinian Jews engaged in three disastrous military revolts from Rome in AD 66-135. These decimated the nation and greatly reduced their national, cultural, and religious identity and influence within the Roman Empire. None of the Apostolic Fathers were Jewish, nor any of the noted early church fathers. After the first century, Jewish leadership involvement and impact within Christendom tapered off significantly. Throughout the theological discourses and debates of the church councils of the fourth and fifth centuries, there was no identifiable input from Jewish Christians. Their ideas and perspectives were not sought. Their voice was silent.

This was in part because the Jews were considered to be theologically misguided or ignorant, having nothing of value to offer. After all, hadn't Jesus said they were "foolish...and slow to believe..." (Luke 24:25)? Hadn't they rejected and crucified their Messiah? There was strong anti-semitism at the time as, for example, reflected in this decree from the Council of Laodicea of AD 364: "Christians must not Judaize by resting on the Sabbath...if any are found to be

---

1. Robert Hach, *Possession and Persuasion: The Rhetoric of Christian Faith* (Miami: Xlibris, 2001), 120.

Judaizing let them be declared anathema from Christ."[2]

Even though the New Testament is written in Greek, its thought forms and cultural background are very Hebrew. In his book *The Distinctive Ideas of the Old Testament*, N.H. Snaith concludes: "Our position is that the reinterpretation of Biblical theology in terms of the ideas of the Greek philosophers has been both widespread throughout the centuries and everywhere destructive to the essence of the Christian faith."[3] The result of this cultural and intellectual drift was that the simple biblical narrative of the Jewish Messiah got lost in a world of Greek metaphysical thought and theological speculation.

2. Greek vs Hebrew Worldview

> Do your best to present yourself to God as one approved, a worker who does not need to be ashamed and who correctly handles the word of truth. (2 Tim. 2:15)

There is a science to "correctly handling the word of truth"—to interpreting and understanding the Bible (or any literary work), called "hermeneutics." It's not rocket science. Most of the principles and rules are common sense. But we ignore them to our detriment. Two key principles have to do with our assumptions and the context:

First, we need to be careful that we do not assume that the author's worldview, beliefs, and perspectives are the same as ours, nor that he or she shares the same understanding and usage in the words or terms employed. We also need to be aware of our preconceived ideas or theologies. Do they naturally arise out of, or align with, the text, or are we imposing them upon the text and interpreting it to say what we want it to say?

Second, we need to allow the context to shape and inform the meaning of what is being communicated—the literary context, the situational context, and the wider cultural context. What is the overall

2. Karl Joseph Hefele, *A History of the Councils of the Church: from the Original Documents, to the close of the Second Council of Nicaea A.D. 787* (Eugene, OR: Wipf & Stock Pub, 2007), 316.

3. N. H. Snaith, *The Distinctive Ideas of the Old Testament* (Philadelphia: Westminster Press, 1946), 187.

flow of ideas and consistency of thought patterns within these contexts? As someone expressed it, "A text without a context is a pretext!" To state it more bluntly: "If you take a text out of its context, you're left with a 'con'."

Unfortunately, the vast majority of church leaders and theologians of the early post-New Testament period, because of their non-Hebrew thinking or anti-Hebrew bias, basically ignored or disregarded the cultural context of the Bible. Little consideration was given as to how the original Jewish writers thought or expressed their ideas and to how the original audience would have heard them or read what they wrote.

This is evidenced by the allegorical interpretation of Scripture that came into vogue among theologians in the early centuries of the church. This interpretative approach was heavily influenced by Greek philosophy and mysticism. It focused on the spiritual or metaphysical concepts and hidden symbolic meanings behind what was written, while often ignoring the historical context or dismissing the literal meaning as of little importance.

Origen's explanation of the Good Samaritan in Luke 10 is an example: in his interpretation, the man who is robbed is Adam, Jerusalem is paradise, and Jericho is the world.[4] The priest is the Law and the Levites are the Prophets. The Samaritan is Christ. The donkey is Christ's physical body, which bears the burden of the wounded man (the wounds are his sins), and the inn is the Church. The Samaritan's promise to return is a promise of the second coming of Christ.

Ignoring the Hebraic culture, literary style, and historical context led to misunderstandings that persist to this day. Let me give four examples that are particularly relevant to Trinitarian theology:

THE PRINCIPLE OF AGENCY

In Matthew 8:5-13 we have the account of a Centurion coming

---

4. Origen, *Homilies on Luke* trans. Joseph T. Lienhard, (Washington, D.C.: CUA Press, 1996), 136.

to Jesus, requesting that the Lord heal his suffering servant. The conversation that ensues is directly between the soldier and Jesus. Luke's account of the same incident (Luke 7:1-10) says that the Centurion never actually came to Jesus personally, but rather he sent some Jewish elders who pleaded his case for him.

Was it the Centurion or the elders who interacted with Jesus? What's going on here, a contradiction between two Gospel accounts? I believe the difference is easily appreciated when we understand the principle of agency, which Matthew assumes and utilizes from his Jewish background, but which Luke doesn't employ because of his gentile culture and intended Greek recipient, Theophilus. The Jewish elders were acting as the Centurian's agents—fully representing him as though he himself were present.

Today, we have a limited exposure to this principle through legal appointments such as an "Agent" or "Power of Attorney," where someone is authorized to act on their client's behalf in negotiations or even signing of documents. But in Hebrew or ancient Middle-Eastern thinking, this goes to a whole different level.

In that culture the agent fully represented the one on whose behalf they were acting, so that the two are identified as one and the same person. The one sent is identified as the one he or she represents, and so is seen, treated, and responded to accordingly. As expressed in *The Encyclopedia of Jewish Religion*: "Agent (Heb. *Shaliach*): The main point of the Jewish law of agency is expressed in the dictum, 'a person's agent is regarded as the person himself.'"[5]

Other examples abound in the Scriptures. Here are but a few:

- JACOB'S WRESTLE. Jacob struggled with "a man" until dawn, yet said he "saw God face to face" (Gen 32:24-30). Hosea comments: "As a man he [Jacob] struggled with God; he struggled with the angel and overcame him" (Hosea 12:3-4).
- MOSES BEFORE THE BURNING BUSH. "God" calls to

---

5. R. J. Zwi Werblowsky, *Encyclopedia of the Jewish Religion* rev. ed., ed. Geoffrey Widoger, (London: Phoenix House, 1996), 15.

Moses and says, "I am the God of your father, the God of Abraham, the God of Isaac and the God of Jacob" (Exod. 3:4-6). He later declares, "I Am Who I Am. This is what you are to say to the Israelites: 'I Am has sent me to you'" (v. 14). Yet we are told quite plainly that "the angel of the Lord appeared to him in flames of fire from within a bush" (Exod. 3:2). Stephen also reflects this Jewish understanding of agency in his description of the event (Acts 7:31-33).

- ISRAEL'S JUDGES. Exodus 21:6 reads in some translations, "Then his master shall bring him to the judges,"[6] and in other translations, "His master shall bring him to God."[7] Because the judges are representing God as his agents they are actually called "God" (Hebrew: *Elohim*).
- A MOTHER'S REQUEST. In Matthew 20:20-22 and Mark 10:35-37 we have two accounts of the same incident. In Mark's account James and John ask Jesus directly for places of honor in his coming kingdom. In Matthew, it is their mother who asks on their behalf.

A conservative Jewish Rabbi was once explaining to me the many laws and rules that surround their Sabbath rest. For example, they can't cook or even light a fire because such activities are considered to be work. On the same basis, they walk to the synagogue to worship—driving a car is forbidden because the spark of the internal combustion engine is seen as lighting a fire, and hence viewed as work. I asked the obvious question: "Well, can't you just take a taxi?" His response demonstrated that the principle of agency still operates in traditional Jewish culture today: "To commission somebody else to drive for me is as though I were driving myself. I would be guilty of breaking the law."

There is a common Trinitarian argument that because Jesus performed the works foretold that God would do among his people, it

---

6. See KJV, NIV.

7. See NASB, RSV.

demonstrated he was God. Jesus did what only God can do, therefore he must be God. Right observation, but wrong conclusion. As we've seen, what it demonstrates is that God was at work in and through Jesus. Christ was God's authorized representative—his agent, speaking and acting on his Father's behalf. Or as Peter expressed it in his first gospel sermon on the day of Pentecost: "Jesus of Nazareth was a man accredited by God to you by miracles, wonders and signs, which God did among you through him..." (Acts 2:22).

The Trinitarian argument uses examples such as Jesus healing the paralyzed man lowered through the roof by his friends (Mark 2:1-12). In response to their faith, Jesus declared to the man on the stretcher: "Son, your sins are forgiven" (v. 5). The religious leaders jumped on that statement, making it out to be blasphemous: "Who can forgive sins but God alone?" (v. 7). Jesus' response, however, backed up by his miracle of healing, was to prove "that the Son of Man has authority on earth to forgive sins" (v. 10). The crowd certainly came to the same conclusion. They "were filled with awe; and they praised God, who had given such authority to man" (Matt. 9:8).

Similarly, when the villagers at Nain witnessed Jesus' miracle of raising a dead person back to life, their response was, "A great prophet has appeared among us...God has come to help his people" (Luke 7:16). Again, this is a clear statement of their concept of prophetic agency: "God has come," equates to, "a great prophet has appeared among us."

Jesus was constantly acting on behalf of his Father and by his Father's authority. Consider the following statements:

> Whoever believes in me does not believe in me only, but in the one who sent me. The one who looks at me is seeing the one who sent me...whatever I say is just what the Father has told me to say. (John 12:44-45, 50)

> Don't you know me, Philip, even after I have been among you such a long time? Anyone who has seen me has seen the Father. How can you say, "Show us the Father"? Don't you believe that I am in the Father, and that the Father is in me?

> The words I say to you I do not speak on my own authority.
> Rather, it is the Father, living in me, who is doing his work.
> (John 14:9-10)

> I give them eternal life, and they shall never perish; no one
> will snatch them out of my hand. My Father, who has given
> them to me, is greater than all; no one can snatch them out
> of my Father's hand. I and the Father are one. (John 10:28-
> 30)

Such statements are often interpreted ontologically—as expressions of Jesus' deity. But closer examination shows that Jesus is not saying here and elsewhere that he is the Father or that they share the same essence. The distinction between them is always maintained, yet at the same time Jesus fully identifies with, represents, and expresses the Father's interests and intentions, words and ways, character and claims. He and the Father are completely harmonized and totally aligned in every way—in heart, word, action, will, and purpose, so that Jesus uniquely and completely expresses his Father on earth. He is God's ultimate revelation, reflection, and representative.

Acting with divine agency, Jesus shares in the authority and prerogatives of the Father: to judge the world at the end of the age (Matt. 25:31); to give life (John 6:33) and resurrect those who belong to him (John 6:44); to be glorified along with the Father (Luke 9:26); and so forth.

In the Gospel account, Jesus commissioned 72 of his disciples and sent them out as his agents, representing him: "Whoever listens to you listens to me; whoever rejects you rejects me; but whoever rejects me rejects him who sent me" (Luke 10:16).

The commission and agency from the Father to Jesus also operated through him to his disciples (Matt. 28:18-20). Appreciating this principle not only clarifies Jesus' nature, calling, and authority, but also ours in him.

THE JEWISH CONCEPT OF PREEXISTENCE

A friend of mine completely restored and refurbished a historic house and added on some extra rooms and features. It now functions beautifully as a preschool daycare center.

Not far from where I live, a purpose-built daycare center has just been erected. The architect had the overall purpose in mind, was given a design brief, and drew up plans that were submitted for developmental approval. From these, construction plans were detailed and a contract with a builder was signed. This all took place before anything happened physically on the site and the building began to materialize.

In both of these cases, it could be said that the daycare center "preexisted." In the first instance, it preexisted in an actual and physical sense as a house. In the second it preexisted as a concept and intention before ever materializing. Before its construction, the owner, architect, planners and builders would all speak about the daycare center as though it were real—long before its actual existence.

When it comes to interpreting the Scriptures, most people adopt a Western understanding of preexistence generally, and of Jesus specifically, without ever realizing that the Hebrew understanding was very different. Trinitarian theologians assume a personal or actual preexistence. But the Hebrew understanding was *intentional* and *notional*.

For the Jews, God is the supreme architect, who conceived and purposed events, people, and realities before they ever came to be in an actual or material sense. This is reflected in many of their writings, such as the Babylonian Talmud, compiled in AD 500, but with sayings that go back to as early as the New Testament apostolic period. It gives a good insight into Jewish thinking during that period:

> Seven things were created before the world was made, and these are they: Torah, repentance, the Garden of Eden, Gehenna, the throne of glory, the house of the sanctuary, and the name of the Messiah.
>
> Torah: "The Lord possessed me in the beginning of his way, before the works of old." (Prov. 8:22)

Repentance: "Before the mountains were brought forth, or even [before] you had formed the earth and the world... you turn man to destruction and say, Repent, you sons of men." (Ps. 90:2)

The Garden of Eden: "And the Lord God planted a garden in Eden from aforetime." (Gen. 2:8)

Gehenna: "For Tophet is ordained from old." (Isa. 30:33)

The throne of glory: "Your throne is established from of old." (Ps. 93:2)

The house of the sanctuary: "A glorious high throne from the beginning is the place of your sanctuary." (Jer. 17:12)

And the name of the Messiah: "His name shall endure forever and has existed before the sun" (Ps. 72:17). (b.Pes 54a; b.Ned 39b)

Note that this list includes both material and non-material realities. Significantly, it includes the name of the Messiah—not the person, but *messianic notional preexistence*. The *Genesis Rabbah* has a similar list and many other ancient Hebrew texts could be referenced. Peter's address on the Day of Pentecost reflects this Jewish understanding when he says Jesus was "handed over...by God's deliberate plan and foreknowledge" (Acts 2:23).

We know Jesus was crucified around AD 30, yet the Scriptures say he "was slain from the creation of the world" (Rev. 13:8), and that Jesus was chosen as the sacrificial lamb before the world was made (1 Pet. 1:20). The Bible teaches that God promised us eternal life "before the beginning of time" (Titus 1:2), that we were chosen in Christ "before the creation of the world" (Eph. 1:4), and that God's plan for our glorification was "before time began" (1 Cor. 2:7). These things did not happen physically, but intentionally in the plan and purposes of God from the very outset: a notional and conceptual preexistence.

Just as a building always has a conceptual preexistence before its physical existence, so it is with the things of God. The tabernacle was according to the design that God showed Moses on the mountain. It was "a copy and shadow of what is in heaven" (Heb. 8:5). In this same sense, Paul says we already "have [past tense] a building from God"—our resurrection body "in heaven" that we have yet to receive (2 Cor. 5:1).

An interesting example is when Jesus prays in John 17:5, "And now, Father, glorify me in your presence with the glory I had with you before the world began." Usually a physical preexistence is assumed here, with Jesus literally present with God in heaven before creation. But given the Hebraic understanding of preexistence, it is much more likely conceptual, not physical. In fact, Jesus goes on to say that believers have been given that same glory—even those not yet born or physically existing (John 17:20-22).

We have a God who "calls into being things that were not" (Rom. 4:17), or "calls into existence the things that do not exist" (NRSV). In fact, the plans and purposes of God are so certain that they are often written "proleptically," as though they have already happened. For example, Isaiah's prophecies about the suffering and glory of the coming Messiah (Isa. 52:13—53:12) are all written in the past tense, even though their fulfillment was then a long time in the future:

> Surely he took up our pain and bore our suffering,
> Yet we considered him punished by God,
> stricken by him, and afflicted.
> But he was pierced for our transgressions,
> he was crushed for our iniquities;
> the punishment that brought us peace was on him,
> and by his wounds we are healed. (Isa. 53:4-5)

Trinitarians believe that Jesus is fully God and must therefore be eternal, and to have actually existed as a person prior to his birth in Bethlehem. This is the assumption they bring to their understanding when speaking of his "preexistence," but is this the scriptural understanding? Although we'll consider this later, it's sufficient to note for now that a different kind of preexistence is understood in Hebraic thinking and writings, including the Old and New Testaments.

Words Denoting Deity

There is a flexibility in meaning and a fluidity in understanding for "God" and "Lord" within the biblical text that can be easily overlooked when reading the Bible in English. This is exacerbated by the fact that the Greek language has only one word for "God" (*Theos*) and one word for "Lord" (*Kurios*), whereas the Hebrew has more than one for each, as below:

God

Not a personal name, God is rather a title or defining noun. In the Old Testament there are two main names by which Israel's God is called: *Yahweh* and *Elohim*.

Yahweh is God's self-designation and personal name expressed to Moses at the burning bush—the Hebrew tetragrammaton ("four letters") of *YHWH*, to which vowels are added to make *Yahweh*, (or Jehovah). This name roughly means "I am," or more accurately "I will be." It is used prolifically in the Old Testament, some 6,828 times, and is the name by which God himself wishes to be uniquely known and proclaimed: "This is my name forever, the name you shall call me from generation to generation" (Exod. 3:15).

The second is *Elohim*, which is more of a title than a personal name—hence, the combination *Yahweh Elohim* ("LORD God" in most Bibles) occurs 891 times. *Elohim* appears some 2,602 times in the Old Testament Scriptures. About 15 percent of its usage is not in relation to *Yahweh*, but to idols and false gods (e.g., Exod. 12:12; 32:4; 1 Kings 11:33) or to humans and angels (e.g., Exod. 4:16; 7:1; Ps. 82:6). In this sense it's similar to the title "Majesty" which is used of God (Heb. 1:3; 8:1) but also people of esteem: "Your Majesty, the King" (e.g., 1 Sam. 17:55; 23:20; 2 Chron. 25:7).

Lord

This is also a title of respect (like "majesty") and likewise can be conferred upon God or upon humans. The two different words for "Lord" in the Hebrew Old Testament text are designated and distinguished by different Masoretic vowel pointings.

The Hebrew name for God, *YHWH*, is generally translated as "LORD" with all capital letters. *Adonai* is the Hebrew word for "Lord" when it refers to *YHWH* and is designated by a capital "L" followed by lower case (Lord). It appears 449 times in the Old Testament, and only ever refers to the LORD God of Israel. On the other hand, the 195 times when *Adoni* ("lord" or "my lord") is used, it is *never* a divine reference, but is only ever applied to humans (or occasionally to angels). These distinctions are often, but not always, preserved with the differing forms of the word for "lord" in our English translations.

The following are just a couple of many examples where the word "Lord" is used in both senses, side by side:

> So Sarah laughed to herself as she thought, "After I am worn out and my lord is old, will I now have this pleasure?" Then the LORD said to Abraham... (Gen. 18:12-13)

> "Drink, my lord," she said... Without saying a word, the man watched her closely to learn whether or not the LORD had made his journey successful. (Gen. 24:18, 21)

An important text where this distinction is crucial is Psalm 110:1, where David says, "The LORD says to my lord: 'Sit at my right hand until I make your enemies a footstool for your feet.'" This is the most quoted Old Testament verse in the New Testament, and therefore a key to understanding the Christology of the New Testament writers. It was used by Jesus to prove that the Messiah is not only King David's descendant, but his lord and superior (Matt. 22:41-46).

The first LORD in the verse is the Hebrew for *Yahweh*. The second is *Adoni*, which necessarily refers to David's human lord, the Messiah. This verse accords with the New Testament teaching of the

Father's exaltation of Jesus to his right hand, where "God placed all things under his feet" (Eph. 1:22). The salient point here is that the two different "Lords" used in the Hebrew text in this verse unambiguously and unequivocally put Jesus on a distinctly different level from Almighty God. This aligns with the consistent understanding of the Messiah in both the Old Testament and the New Testament.

In translation from the Hebrew to Greek, (as in the Septuagint, or LXX), and again from Greek to English, the difference between these two "Lords" must be distinguished carefully. Conventional usage and context will determine whether the text refers to a human or divine Lord.

A key verse where this applies is John 20:28, when Thomas declares to the resurrected Christ, "My Lord and my God!" In what sense is he using these titles? This verse is examined in Appendix A.

In the New Testament...

- The word "God" (Greek: *Theos*) is used over 1,300 times.
- Someone other than *Yahweh* can be called by this title. Satan is called "the god of this age" (2 Cor. 4:4).
  Foreign deities or idols are called "gods" (e.g., Acts 7:40; 14:11; 17:18; 19:26; 28:11; 1 Cor. 8:5) and along these lines even one's stomach can be "god" (Phil. 3:19). Interestingly, the only man who "proclaim[s] himself to be God" (2 Thess. 2:4) is the antichrist, "the man of lawlessness" (2 Thess. 2:3).
- Jesus is only clearly called "God" twice in the whole New Testament (John 20:28; Heb. 1:8). I believe that when both the context and fluidity of terminology are considered, these exceptions are easily explained. These and a couple of disputed texts (Rom. 9:5; Titus 2:13; 2 Pet. 1:2) will be considered in Appendix A.
- Outside these few exceptions, whenever God is referred to or qualified, the New Testament authors *always* call him the "Father." He is further identified and distinguished from Jesus many times, with such statements as "the God and

Father of our Lord Jesus Christ" (Rom. 15:6; 2 Cor. 1:3; Eph. 1:3; 1 Pet. 1:3).[8]

- God is seen as a single person, with single verbs, nouns, and pronouns *always* used of him (e.g., "May God himself..." 1 Thess. 5:23). In Galatians 3:20, Paul states clearly that "God is one." Here, "one," is masculine in the Greek, so he is saying that God is one person, not entity or trinity. Paul calls on God as his singular "witness" (Rom. 1:9; 2 Cor. 1:23) even when his argument would have been better served if he could have appealed to God as being more than one (Deut. 19:15; 2 Cor. 13:1). In short, there is no clear evidence that the New Testament authors conceived of God as anyone other than *Yahweh*, who is identified as the Father, and is consistently seen as distinct from Jesus.[9]

- Many times Jesus is referred to as "Lord," a term used interchangeably with "Messiah" and "Son of God" (e.g., Matt. 15:22; 22:42; 26:63; Luke 2:11; John 11:27; Rom. 8:1-4; 1 John 5:1-5). Because Jesus is seen as God's anointed and sovereign king, for Christians in imperial Rome at the time to claim him as their lord was a clear statement of their allegiance. They were rejecting Caesar, the deified King of the Empire, as their lord, and proclaiming Jesus as their king.

- There is no legitimate basis, as claimed by some, that Jesus' title of "Lord" is a conferring of deity upon him. In fact, he is often called "our Lord" or "your Lord" (Rom. 1:4; 5:1, 11, 21; 7:25; 8:39, etc.). These possessive expressions are never used of "the LORD" (*Yahweh*) in the Old Testament.

- Paul and others use the title "Lord" for Jesus, not to identify

8. See also Eph. 1:17; Col. 1:3; 1 Thess. 3:13.

9. To consider further evidence of Paul's clear distinction between Jesus and God, see "Podcast 225 – Biblical Words for God and for his Son Part 2 – Old 'Lord' vs. New 'Lord'" by Dale Tuggy, *Trinities*, April 29, 2018, https://trinities.org/blog/podcast-225-biblical-words-for-god-and-for-his-son-part-2-old-lord-vs-new-lord/.

him as God, but rather to distinguish him from God
(Rom. 15:6; 16:27; 1 Cor. 8:6; 15:24-28; 2 Cor. 1:3; 11:31;
Eph. 1:3, 17; Phil. 2:11; Col. 1:3, etc.).

> There is one body and one Spirit—just as you were called to
> the one hope that belongs to your call—*one Lord*, one faith,
> one baptism, *one God* and Father of all, who is over all and
> through all and in all. (Eph. 4:4-6; emphasis added)

Wisdom Personified

Wisdom literature features in the Old Testament, specifically in Job, Proverbs, and Ecclesiastes, but is also scattered through the Psalms and prophetic books. In the post-exilic period of Israel's history, there was a strong emphasis on observance of the Law (*Torah*) along with the concept of Wisdom. This torah-centered wisdom tradition was developed and expressed in a number of Intertestamental books such as Sirach, Baruch, Wisdom of Solomon, and the writings of Philo.

Much of this material was included in the Septuagint and was well known to the authors of the New Testament. Many biblical scholars have noted the degree to which these authors allude to, or incorporate, this wisdom material into their writings. Exploring Wisdom Christology is beyond the scope of our discussion. However, here are some key things to note about how Wisdom was described at the time:

- Wisdom had a divine origin.[10]
- Wisdom existed before creation and had an active role in creation.[11]
- Wisdom had a redemptive mission to human beings.[12]

---

10. Prov. 8:22; Ecclus. 24:3; Wisd. of Sol. 7:25-26.

11. Prov. 8:22-29; Ecclus. 1:4; Wisd. of Sol. 9:9; Prov. 8:30; 3:19; Ecclus. 1:9-10; Wisd. of Sol. 7:22; 8:4-6.

12. Prov. 8:4; 31-36; Ecclus. 24:7, 12, 19-22; Wisd. of Sol. 7:27-28; 8:2-3.

- Wisdom was interconnected with God's instructive counsel, and therefore his laws and precepts, his Torah.[13]
- Wisdom was a gift from God of supreme worth.[14]
- Wisdom was portrayed as a person.[15]

On this last point: personification is a literary device where inanimate objects or concepts are endowed with human characteristics and attributes. It is frequently employed in the Bible, especially in figurative or poetic literature. Personifications could be expressed or embodied in certain individuals, such as wisdom in the wife of noble character (Prov. 31), Abraham's wife Sarah (Wisd. of Sol. 11), or Simon the High Priest (Ecclus. 50).

However, personifications of wisdom or of God's law never become actual people—Judaism's strict monotheism would never allow this. For example, even though God's "word" (Hebrew: *dabar*) is personified many times in the Old Testament (e.g., Pss. 33:6; 147:15; Jer. 23:29), of the 1,455 times it occurs, it never becomes a conscious person. It was never the intention of the authors using personification that the reader would conceive of the personified Word as a literal person.

One well known example of Wisdom personified appears in Proverbs chapters 8 and 9, where Wisdom is seen as a woman who calls out and beckons people to seek her and find the reward that is to be gained from her. Lady Wisdom also declares:

> The LORD brought me forth as the first of his works,
>   before his deeds of old;
> I was formed long ages ago,
>   at the very beginning, when the world came to be.
> ...I was there when he set the heavens in place...
>   then I was constantly at his side.
> I was filled with delight day after day,

13. Job 28:20-28; Prov. 3:19-20; Ecclus. 24; Bar. 3:9-4:4; Wisd. of Sol. 7-9.

14. Prov. 2:6; 8-9; Ecclus. 1:9-10, 26; 6:37; Wisd. of Sol. 7:7; 9:4.

15. Job 28; Prov. 1, 8, 9; Ecclus. 1:9-10; 4:11-19; 6:18-31; 14:20-15:8; 51:13-21; Bar. 3:9-4:4; Wisd. of Sol. 6:12-11:1.

> rejoicing always in his presence,
> rejoicing in his whole world
> and delighting in mankind. (Prov. 8:22-23, 27, 30-31)

The same thought is expressed earlier in chapter 3: "By wisdom the LORD laid the earth's foundations, by understanding he set the heavens in place; by his knowledge the watery depths were divided, and the clouds let drop the dew" (Prov. 3:19-20). In Hebrew poetry, as here, identical or similar thoughts are placed in parallel, so God's wisdom, understanding, and knowledge are grouped as synonymous and applied to his powerful and creative word, as seen in the Genesis account with the frequently repeated phrase, "And God said..." (Gen. 1).

Given the above, it's easy to see how the New Testament authors saw Jesus as taking on the persona and role of wisdom. After all, Jesus declared "something greater than Solomon is here" (Matt. 12:42; Luke 11:31). Paul proclaims Christ as "the power of God and the wisdom of God," the one "who has become for us wisdom from God" (1 Cor. 1:24, 30). The writer to the Hebrews takes rare terminology from personified Wisdom literature to describe Jesus as God's "radiance" (*apaugasma*) and "imprint" (*xarakter*). As with Wisdom, Jesus is seen as a throne companion of God (Luke 22:69; Acts 7:55; Rom. 8:34; 1 Pet. 3:22, etc.).

The New Testament writers present Jesus as the climactic embodiment of God's personified Word and Wisdom. Everything formerly said about Wisdom is applied to Jesus, he being its ultimate expression. And understanding the active role and involvement of Wisdom in God's initial creation, it's not difficult to see how Paul employs this in expressing Christ's role in bringing about God's new creation (1 Cor. 8:6; Col. 1:15-17).

It also helps us understand personified Wisdom as portrayed in the *logos* poem of John's prologue to his Gospel (1:1-18). If "wisdom is best understood in her Biblical expression as a communication of

God,"[16] we can see how and why John uses "*logos*" to refer to Jesus. He presents the Messiah as the culmination of God's Word, his wise and good intention for his people, superceding the place of Wisdom and Torah as the embodied and ultimate revelation of God:

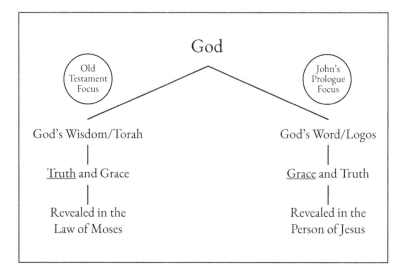

(This prologue is discussed further in Appendix A.)

3. The Power of Paradigms

Karl Popper and Thomas Kuhn introduced the concept of conflict thinking into our understanding of the philosophy and methodology of science.[17] Kuhn believed that scientific investigation normally proceeds within an accepted theory (or a paradigm), governed by an agreed world-view and set of assumptions shared by the scientific community.

However, occasionally an anomaly will arise, sparked by a novel invention or discovery of new facts, that challenges the existing

16. Roland Murphy, *The Tree of Life: An Exploration of Biblical Wisdom Literature* (Grand Rapids, MI: Eerdmans, 2002), 33.

17. Thomas S. Kuhn, *The Structure of Scientific Revolutions*, 3rd ed. (Chicago: The University of Chicago Press, 1996).

paradigm. This creates a crisis, which may lead to a "revolution," a change of paradigm and establishment of a new theory. Some examples are Copernicus' heliocentric cosmology (the earth goes around the sun) overcoming the established Aristotelian model (everything revolves around the earth); Quantum Theory and Einstein's Theory of Relativity superseding Newtonian physics; and the Big Bang Theory now in vogue over the once dominant Steady State Theory.

A salient point Kuhn makes is that once people are in a paradigm, it's very difficult to get out of it. Transitions in scientific paradigms don't happen easily—that's why he called them revolutions. Paradigms inherently contain a restriction of vision, a rigid methodology, and an accepted set of assumptions and rules. They are notoriously resistant to change.

If that is true of scientific paradigms, how much more is it true of theological paradigms, where we are dealing not just with objective facts, but beliefs that reach deep into our spirit and psyche. I had grown up singing Trinitarian hymns that spoke of such things as "God in three persons, blessed Trinity" and many modern worship songs that address Jesus as God. There was a significant spiritual, psychological, and emotional dimension to my belief in the deity of Jesus.

Kuhn proposes that another reason paradigms are so resistant to change is that the scientific community upholds and reinforces them. Traditions are revered, power politics is at play, scientific leaders are personally invested, income and reputations are at stake, and so variant views are rejected. There is pressure to conform. All of this is no less applicable, and even more pronounced, in the theological community.

My doctrinal transition was a paradigm shift, and I experienced the inherent resistance that comes with such a crisis. I remember the struggle as I read different books on the subject. If the author was Non-trinitarian, my response to the arguments were typically, "Yes, but..." or, "Okay, but what about....?" The turning point from this impasse came when one day I decided to read the New Testament, not through my usual "Trinitarian lens," but a traditional monotheistic and Jewish one, where the man Jesus was the Messiah, the Son of God, but not himself God.

I was amazed at how much more simply and clearly it read. There was no need to engage in internal mental gymnastics in order for the text to make sense. This new paradigm was exegetically and theologically a better fit.

4. Translation

Our English translations of the Hebrew and Greek texts are generally accurate and reliable. This will vary a little between versions, with some more faithfully adhering to a literal transposition while others are more interpretive in their prose (often to make the text more readable or contemporary in expression and understanding). However, given our Western cultural heritage, historical biases, and current theological paradigms, it would be unrealistic to assume that these have not been at play and had some influence, albeit unwittingly, in the work of the biblical scholars who have done the translating.

Scribes reproducing documents and scholars later translating them were susceptible on occasion to making them say what they were already thought to mean. Sometimes external pressure was also brought to bear, with church or state politics having a part to play. Below are a few examples:

After the Hampton Court Conference in AD 1604, King James commissioned the English translation that bears his name. Fourteen edicts were mandated to the translators. Edict number three was that the Greek word *ekklesia* must be translated "church," not "congregation" or "assembly" (its normal or natural meaning). Apparently the king wanted to shore up the stability and authority of church and state, and hence the institution, rather than the people of God, was to be emphasized.

In the same way, the Greek word *baptizo* was not translated as "immerse" or "plunge," which it means, but transliterated. That is, the Greek letters were simply changed to English letters. The reason is obvious: the mode of baptism practiced by the church at the time was christening—sprinkling babies with water—and the ecclesiastical powers did not want this to be challenged.

Because Trinitarian theology was so entrenched in church history prior to English translations of the Scriptures, certain texts that either challenged that doctrine or could be utilized to support it became especially susceptible to translation biases or errors, as Jason BeDuhn notes:

> For the doctrines that Protestantism inherited [from Catholicism] to be considered true, they had to be found in the Bible. And precisely because they were considered true already, there was and is tremendous pressure to read those truths back into the Bible, whether or not they are actually there.[18]

He therefore notes that...

> The Reformation fought for the access of all believers to the Bible and the right of the individual to directly encounter and interpret the text. Modern translators undermine that cause when they publish interpretations rather than translations, still trying to direct readers to the understanding acceptable to the beliefs and biases of the translators themselves.[19]

Here are a few examples relating to Trinitarian doctrine:

- JOHN 1:1 "In the beginning was the Word..." There is no textual reason for "word" to be capitalized. It wasn't differentiated in the original manuscripts. There isn't any precedent for it in the Old Testament, nor is the word personalized elsewhere. It shows the bias of the translators, who simply presume it refers to a literal preexistent Christ.
- JOHN 13:3 "Jesus ... had come from God and was returning to God." Here the Greek text does not say that Jesus was

---

18. Jason David BeDuhn, *Truth in Translation* (Lanham, MD: University Press of America, 2003), 163.

19. ibid., 48.

"returning" to God, but rather "going" to God (*upagei*). Greek has a perfectly appropriate word, an exact term, for "returning" or "going back": *hypostrepho*. The translators have ignored this for no apparent reason other than their theological bias. The same error is repeated in John 16:28 and John 20:17, depending on the version.

- PHILIPPIANS 2:6 "...who, being in very nature God." Given its usual meaning and exclusive usage in the Bible,[20] the Greek expression *morphe theou* is best translated as "form of God," focusing on outer appearance or shape.[21] Many translations lean toward a more unlikely "essence" or "nature" translation in keeping with their Trinitarian paradigm. Some translations take the liberty of pushing it even further: "though he was God" (TLB), "Christ was truly God" (CEV), and so forth, which is not at all what the Greek text says.

- MATTHEW 24:36 "But about that day or hour no one knows, not even the angels in heaven, nor the Son, but only the Father." Here the words "nor the Son" are omitted in later manuscripts and in many of our English translations— to mask the fact that Jesus is not all-knowing.

- 1 CORINTHIANS 10:9 "We should not test Christ, as some of them did—and were killed by snakes." Here, "Christ" is substituted for "Lord." Again, in Jude 1:5, translators trade "Jesus" for "the Lord" in some translations. Reputable Trinitarian scholars acknowledge these as deliberate alterations to make it appear as though Jesus Christ was personally present in the Old Testament.

---

20. e.g., LXX; Job 4:15-16; Isa. 44:13; Dan. 3:19; Matt. 17:2; Mark 9:2, 16:12; 2 Cor. 3:18.

21. For further discussion, see "A reading of Philippians 2:5-11," by Dale Tuggy, *Trinities*, July 31, 2019, https://trinities.org/blog/a-reading-of-philippians-25-11/.

Others could be added, and we'll encounter more in chapter 5 and Appendix A, but this is a good start.

Summary:

In hindsight, it's not difficult to see how the Trinitarian theological construct developed and has persisted. I'm not suggesting a conspiracy theory, that it was preplanned and deliberately engineered. Rather, it came about consequentially, as the result of a pervasive cultural and intellectual drift that resulted in the Bible no longer being read in its Hebraic cultural context, but reshaped through a Greek philosophical perspective. Once the paradigm was established, it became further embedded and entrenched by church culture and by biases in translation and interpretation.

My hope is that understanding the above will enable us to be a little more objective—able to approach the Scriptures with fresh eyes, an open mind, and a teachable spirit. Ultimately it's not history, tradition, ecclesiastical authority or scholastic opinion we turn to. It comes back to this: what does the Bible say about who Jesus is? That is what we will now consider.

CHAPTER 5

WHAT DOES THE BIBLE TEACH?

THE FOLLOWING IS A brief overview of the biblical witness as to the person and nature of God, especially as it relates to Trinitarian versus Non-trinitarian perspectives. Some contentious passages are left out of this discussion and are dealt with in Appendix A, so that...

- We don't get bogged down in technical detail.
- We don't just focus on the exceptions or those passages that have been heavily biased by translation or interpretation.
- We can give passages more thorough consideration.
- We get the big picture of what the Bible teaches, framing the context for better understanding of individual verses or passages.

Whether you are seeking biblical support for a Trinitarian or Non-trinitarian position, you'll find verses and passages that can be used to support your position, as well as others that challenge it. That being said, it is my contention that the case for a Non-trinitarian position is scripturally far more consistent, coherent, and compelling than a Trinitarian one. This is even more strongly so, if you remove translation bias, are willing to consider passages in their literal and cultural context, and reasonably and dispassionately examine the biblical evidence for both positions.

From my perspective, Trinitarian theology relies heavily on a handful of texts which have been translated and / or interpreted to conform to a predetermined theological template. I believe the approach taken in this chapter, that of a contextualized scriptural overview, is a more honest and hermeneutically valid place to start than proof-texting (an approach often adopted by Trinitarians).

Typically, proof-texting is when someone...

- comes to the Scriptures with an agenda or a pre-determined doctrinal position
- selectively looks for those passages that can be used in evidence to support their case, while at the same time ignoring other texts that appear to contradict it
- places the weight of proof on those few selected texts
- ignores the original languages and the immediate literary and wider historical and cultural contexts
- engages in eisegesis rather than exegesis—that is, they interpret and read into the text what they want it to say, rather than fairly and objectively determining what the original author and audience would have understood it to mean.

When constructing a jigsaw puzzle, two things are especially helpful for deciding how to position any individual piece. Firstly, the picture on the box gives an overall perspective. Secondly, by examining more closely the pieces surrounding where it belongs, you can position a given piece more precisely within its context. You then see exactly where and how it fits, contributes to, and completes the whole picture.

Likewise, by firstly getting the overall picture of the Scriptures, it gives us a clearer perspective to better understand individual verses and how they fit into the whole. This chapter provides something of that overview, with Appendix A examining more closely individual texts and contexts—the surrounding pieces, so to speak.

Old Testament

GOD

Key point: The Hebraic faith of the Old Testament Scriptures is strongly, strictly, and thoroughly monotheistic.

Devout Jews would recite the Shema, their foundational statement of faith about God, daily. It began with the declaration: "Hear, O Israel: The LORD our God, the LORD is one" (Deut. 6:4).

This statement is affirmed by Jesus (Matt. 22:34-40; Mark 12:28-34) and is echoed throughout the New Testament (e.g., Rom. 3:30; Gal. 3:20; 1 Cor. 8:6; 1 Tim. 2:5; James 2:9).

There are a few things to note about this declaration. *Echad* is the only word for the number "one" in Hebrew, and it means the same as it does in English: a single entity. Some try to argue that it can be a "compound" unity, involving more than one element. An example often cited is a man and his wife, two people, becoming "one flesh" (Gen. 2:24). This is easily explained—whether it's one flesh, one flock, one nation, one bunch of grapes, or whatever, the "one" refers to the single entity it designates. The plurality of individual elements that comprise that entity are then defined by *a different noun*. Of its 971 occurrences in the Hebrew Scriptures, *Echad* only ever denotes singularity.

The one refers specifically to *Yahweh*. As we've seen, *Yahweh* is the proper and personal name of the one true God, who is understood to be a "person"—a single, personal being, not a force or essence or coalescence of persons.

The Old Testament was translated from Hebrew into Greek from the third century BC by about 70 Jewish scribes. Hence, the Old Testament Greek translation was called the Septuagint (Latin for 70), denoted for brevity by the Roman numerals LXX. Because the scribes involved had such a holy fear of even saying or writing God's name, they translated *Yahweh* as "LORD" (Greek: *Kurios*), a title, rather than his name. While the Jews and New Testament authors understood the connection and distinctions in the Hebrew and LXX texts when referencing *Yahweh*, it later created confusion both for non-Jews and in subsequent Latin and English translations.

In the New Testament, "Lord" may refer to *Yahweh* or to Jesus, and this conflation continues in the church today. Trinitarian doctrine, which typically changed the concept of God from a person to an essence shared by three persons, confused things further.[1] Now the titles "God" and "Lord" are generally used by Christians to refer to any or all of the Father, Son, and Holy Spirit. As we've seen, this is not supported by how these words and titles are used by the New Testament authors.

Many Christians don't even know who *Yahweh* is, except that they may have heard of the iteration "Jehovah," which has a cultish association (as with Jehovah's Witnesses). This is unfortunate, as God wants us to know him personally—as a person—and to be called by his name. After introducing himself by name to Moses at the burning bush, God went on to say, "This is my name forever, the name you shall call me from generation to generation" (Exod. 3:15).

A key point to note is that in every occurrence where *Yahweh* is used in the Old Testament, it is accompanied by singular verbs and pronouns (he, his, him, etc.). Whether it is *Yahweh* speaking of himself, or others speaking of him, this is always the case, without exception.

When *Elohim* (not *Yahweh*) is used, there are a couple of exceptions. On four occasions only (Gen. 1:26; 3:22; 11:7; Isa. 6:8) plural pronouns are used. The most quoted is Genesis 1:26: "Then God said, 'Let us make mankind in our image, in our likeness...'" However, although the pronouns in this statement are plural, the verb translated "said" is singular.

Even Trinitarian scholars (e.g., the NIV Study Bible) interpret this use as God addressing and including the heavenly host who were present (Job 38:7). It is similar to a Formula One driver saying to his support team, "Let's do it! Let's win this race," even though he's the only one driving. Note that in Jesus' commentary on this verse in Matthew 19:4-6, he did not include himself in this creative act:

> "Haven't you read," he replied, "that at the beginning the

---

1. To explore further some of the conceptual and linguistic changes around "God" see "Podcast 226 – Biblical Words for God and for his Son Part 3 – post-biblical uses of biblical words, and new words," by Dale Tuggy, *Trinities*, May 7, 2018, https://trinities.org/blog/podcast-226-biblical-words-for-god-and-for-his-son-part-3-post-biblical-uses-of-biblical-words-and-new-words/.

Creator 'made them male and female'... Therefore what God has joined together, let no one separate."

Some suggest that the title *Elohim* having a plural ending in the Hebrew points to a plurality within God. The Hebrew language does not support this contention, where on many occasions nouns with plural endings are singular in their meaning, such as Sarah's "lives" (Gen. 23:1), Joseph's "faces" (Gen. 16:8, 43), Potiphar as Joseph's "masters" (Gen. 39:2-3), and so forth.

Throughout the Old Testament, the strictest monotheism is upheld at all times. For example, in Isaiah 45 alone it is repeated several times that apart from God, there is no other; there is no god beside him (vv. 5, 15, 18, 21, 22). In short, there is nothing in the Old Testament scriptural texts, or the Hebrew understanding of those texts, which would suggest that God is other than a single being, one person.

JESUS

Key point: The Jewish people have never in their history believed that the Messiah (Christ) is God.

We must understand that Christ is not a title denoting deity. It's the Greek word for "messiah" and means "anointed one." It refers to someone who is authorized by God to represent him and fulfill his purposes in the world. As such, in the Old Testament this designation is used many times of priests (Lev. 4:3, 6, 16; 6:22), kings (1 Sam. 24:6, 10; 2 Sam. 19:21; 2 Chron. 6:42; Isa. 45:1), and even the patriarchs (Ps. 105:15; 1 Chron. 16:22).

Of course, there was an ultimate, future Anointed One, which Moses refered to when he said: "The LORD your God will raise up for you a prophet like me from among you, from your fellow Israelites. You must listen to him" (Deut. 18:15).

It was prophesied of this Messiah that he would be a descendant of David, a man or "son of man" (Ps. 80:17) who would come as *Yahweh*'s chosen and Anointed One to establish God's kingdom on earth. But it would have been inconceivable to the Jews that this ultimate Messiah was *Yahweh*, a part of *Yahweh*, or equal to *Yahweh*.

That would have contravened their strict monotheistic belief.

In the New Testament, "Christ" (Messiah) and "Son of God" frequently appear together as synonymous titles (e.g., Matt. 16:16; 26:63; Mark 1:1; Luke 4:41; John 11:27). The basis for the messianic title "Son of God" comes from Psalm 2:7, where *Yahweh* says "You are my son; today I have become your father." His "anointed" (v. 2) and "King" (v. 6) refer to the future Messiah, whom *Yahweh* installs and establishes on Zion, his "holy mountain," from which the Messiah will reign, not only over Israel but all the nations to the "ends of the earth" (v. 8). Hence, the final exhortation is for world leaders to submit to, revere, and "kiss his son" (v. 12). Just as this Psalm says that the Messiah will come and rule in *Yahweh*'s name, so in the New Testament Jesus says, "I have come in my Father's name" (John 5:43), and speaks of "the works I do in my Father's name" (John 10:25).

Many Christians assume that Jesus being the Son of God is an expression of his deity—in their minds this equates to the title "God the Son." This unfortunate misappropriation is based on an implied analogy—a human son bears the human nature of his father, and the same is assumed to apply to deity. This is not supported by Scripture, where the expression is first applied to the nation Israel (Exod. 4:22; Deut. 32:18), but also applied to God's anointed representatives in the Old Testament (1 Chron. 22:10; Ps. 89:27), to Adam (Luke 3:38), and then to Christians in general (Rom. 8:14-21; Gal. 3:26; 1 John 3:1, etc.). In the Bible, "son of God" is used metaphorically, not metaphysically. It is a relational description, *not an ontological term*.

Not only was "Son of God" a messianic title, but so was Jesus' most frequent self-designation in the Gospels, "son of man." This is a term which...

a. Speaks clearly of Jesus' humanity. In the Old Testament, "son of man" simply means a human being, without exception. It often appears in strict parallel to the word "man" (Isa. 56:2; Jer. 49:18; Ps. 8:4; 80:17; 146:3, etc.).

b. Points to a "special" man within the purposes of God. It had prophetic overtones. In the book of Ezekiel alone it is used over 90 times as a title for the prophet. It also carried kingly or sovereign inference from the end-time vision in Daniel chapter 7:

> In my vision at night I looked, and there before me was one like a son of man, coming with the clouds of heaven. He approached the Ancient of Days and was led into his presence. He was given authority, glory and sovereign power; all nations and peoples of every language worshiped him. His dominion is an everlasting dominion that will not pass away, and his kingdom is one that will never be destroyed. (Dan. 7:13-14)

c.   Disavows deity. The title or expression "son of man" is never used to refer to God in any passage of Scripture. On the contrary, it is quite clearly stated that "God is not a man, that he should lie; neither the son of man, that he should repent..." (Num 23:19, KJV).

Other Scriptures could be cited, but in summary let it be stressed that there is nothing in the Hebrew text of the Old Testament that would suggest that the Messiah is a deity. Rather, as God's Anointed One, he would be a fellow Israelite like Moses, a human descendant of David who would come in *Yahweh*'s name, authorized as his representative, to fulfill *Yahweh*'s saving and redeeming purposes for the world and ultimately usher in God's kingdom on earth, over which he would reign—once again, in *Yahweh*'s name and with his authority.

A common Trinitarian argument is that just as the Jews had not seen or understood some aspects of the prophecies about the Messiah (e.g., his crucifixion and resurrection), they also missed his deity. Hence, they claim that this oversight was addressed and this mystery was revealed and explained in the New Testament. We have already looked at this issue and noted that although there was serious contention and debate surrounding the misunderstood aspects of Jesus' crucifixion, resurrection, and second coming, there is absolute silence when it comes to any controversy about his deity.

What about those times where Jesus supposedly appears in the Old Testament narratives? Some have identified Jesus as "the angel of the Lord" (e.g., Exod. 3:2; Judg. 2:1-4), even though the Bible explicitly teaches that Jesus is not an angel (Heb. 1:1; 2:18). Others perceive Jesus as one of the three "visitors" who appeared to Abraham under the great trees of Mamre (Gen. 18:1), as the man who wrestled with Jacob (Gen. 32:24), as the fourth man in the furnace with Shadrach, Meshach, and Abednego (Dan. 3:25), and so on.

These "Christophanies" are often seen as manifestations of a preincarnate Jesus, but such speculations arise from an assumption of his personal preexistence. There is nothing in the text that indicates this to be the case—nothing that cannot be accounted for by seeing these persons as angels (e.g., Heb. 13:2) acting within the Jewish concept of agency. No New Testament text, rightly understood, portrays Jesus as active in Old Testament times.

Jesus is certainly conceptually and intentionally preexistent throughout the Old Testament. He is present in the plans and purposes of God as expressed in the many prophecies about him. That's why Jesus could say, "before Abraham was born, I am (he)" (John 8:58). Conceptually, as we've seen, not only was Jesus chosen and even "slain from the creation of the world" (Rev. 13:8; see also 1 Pet. 1:20), but he literally appears in the scriptural text before Abraham appears on the scene in Genesis 12—as early as Genesis 3:15: "And I will put enmity between you and the woman, and between your offspring and hers; he will crush your head, and you will strike his heel."

Jesus is also metaphorically present. He is portrayed through the many types, shadows, and allegories that represent him. He is seen in the bronze serpent that was raised up and brought healing and life to those who looked on it (John 3:14), as the manna from heaven that gives life to the world (John 6:33), and as the spiritual rock that gives living water (John 7:37; 1 Cor. 10:6), alongside many others.

One "type" which I find enlightening is that of Joseph as a prefigurement of Christ. Both Joseph and Jesus were dearly loved by their father (Gen. 37:3; Matt. 3:17) and were predestined to save and to rule (Gen. 37:5-7; Luke 2:11). Both were not believed by their brothers

(Gen. 37:8; John 7:5; 15:24). They were both conspired against, stripped, and sold for silver (Gen. 37:23, 28; Matt. 26:15; 27:1, 28). Both were faithful and blameless in their service and were tempted but did not sin (Gen. 39:9; Heb. 4:15). Both were falsely accused (Gen. 39:19-20; Mark 14:56), bound (Gen. 39:30; Matt. 27:2), and condemned with two criminals (Gen. 40:2-3; Luke 23:32)— one of whom was granted life and the other not (Gen. 40:21-22; Luke 23:43). They were both about 30 years old at the time (Gen. 41:46; Luke 3:25). Both were "raised" out of the pit (Gen. 37:28; Eph. 4:9) to the right hand of the sovereign king and given all authority over the kingdom (Gen. 41:41-44; Eph. 1:20-23). In that position they were highly esteemed and worshipped (Gen. 41:43; Matt. 28:17). Their own brothers did not recognize who they were (Gen. 45:1-3; John 1:11), yet upon this revelation there was repentance and reconciliation (Gen. 42:7; Zech. 12:10; Acts 2:38).

Notice that even though Joseph was not Pharaoh, he was highly esteemed by the monarch, appointed to an exalted position, and given all authority to rule over Pharaoh's kingdom: "[God] made me father to Pharaoh, lord of his entire household and ruler of all Egypt" (Gen. 45:8).

Given the many parallels and insights into the life and ministry of Jesus, I wonder: why doesn't this type feature more prominently in Christian teaching today? I suspect that aspects such as Joseph's exaltation, his subordinate relationship under the ultimate sovereign, his designated authority (along with the principle of agency at work), don't quite fit Trinitarian theology. His story is therefore bypassed.

Yes, Jesus does feature prominently in the Old Testament, but not personally or as deity or equal to the Father. He has a conceptual, prophetic, and metaphorical presence rather than a physical one.

One thing is clear—no Jew at the time of Jesus had a Trinitarian perspective on the nature of *Yahweh* or the person of the Messiah. To subsequently read this doctrine back into the Old Testament texts, or to assume that any of the New Testament authors brought such a theological understanding to their writings, is an unsupported assumption.

In fact, we have to assume the exact opposite, that unless the scriptural authors explicitly teach or clearly articulate a doctrinal belief at variance with their religious and cultural heritage at the time, they were working from a Non-trinitarian paradigm. We will now turn to their writings to see if this is the case.

New Testament

Synoptic Gospels

Key point: There is no evidence within the Synoptic Gospels (Matthew, Mark, and Luke) that the authors are trying to portray a deified Christ. In this respect, they hold the classic Hebraic, Old Testament understanding of Almighty God as one person, with a human Messiah under him who fully represents him.

Significantly, the birth accounts, which are only found in Matthew and Luke, point away from any notion of Jesus' personal preexistence. Matthew begins his account with the "genesis" (Greek: *genesis*)—literally, Jesus' beginning or origin (vv. 1, 18). Then the generations are listed from father to son. In all 39 occurrences, the Greek word *egennasen* is used, which means "to beget, to father or sire, to procreate." This is exactly the same word used of Jesus' birth in verse 16.

On the four occasions (vv. 3, 5, 6, 13) where Matthew includes a mother in his list, he uses the Greek word *ek*, which means "out of," as he does of Mary's birth of Jesus (Matt. 1:16). This means Jesus was not born "through" Mary, but was conceived; he originated and began in her womb, and was generated from her as in any normal human birth.

What's unique is Jesus' manner of conception. Here, that which is begotten is literally "from the Holy Spirit" (Matt. 1:20). Luke's account goes into more detail, giving the angel Gabriel's explanation: "The Holy Spirit will come on you, and the power of the Most High will overshadow you. So the holy one to be born will be called the Son of God" (Luke 1:35).

In both accounts there is no definite article before "Spirit."

This absence of a definite article indicates that God's personal presence and power is initiating this new creation. Similar to God's initial creation of the world (Gen. 1:20), God's Spirit hovers over the virgin's void and empty womb to bring forth a new life. There is no hint of an "eternal begetting" here (which is a contradiction in terms), but a begetting at a specific point in time, as confirmed by the rest of Scripture (Ps. 2:7; Heb. 1:5). That's why Jesus is said to be both "born of God" (1 John 5:18) and "born of a woman" (Gal. 4:4).

The Synoptic accounts of Jesus life, teaching, and ministry do not go beyond the foundational testimony that Jesus is "the Messiah, the Son of the living God" (Matt. 16:16; see also Mark 8:28-29; Luke 9:20). It is made clear that Jesus' power and authority are from God, that he is submissive to the Father and dependent on the Father for everything he has (e.g., Matt. 11:27; 15:31; 28:18; Mark 10:18; 11:27-29; Luke 1:32) including his kingdom: "And I confer on you a kingdom, just as my Father conferred one on me" (Luke 22:29).

On one occasion, Jesus said, "Why do you call me good? No one is good—except God alone" (Mark 10:18). The Greek word here for "good" is *agathos*, which means inherently or intrinsically good a quality Jesus declares only fully and appropriately belongs to his Father. All that is truly good derives from him (James 1:17; Rev. 15:3-4).

Also of note in the Synoptic Gospels is Jesus' strong personal endorsement of Israel's strict monotheism. He unequivocally affirms the Shema (Matt. 22:34-40; Mark 12:28-34), including the qualifying statement that "God is one and there is no other but him." He backs this up with his teaching and comments about his Father being the only God (e.g., Matt. 4:10; Luke 18:19; cf. John 5:44; 17:3). How strange it is that Christianity seems to be at variance with its own founder and Lord at the most fundamental level of his understanding of God.

THE GOSPEL OF JOHN

Key point: Many believe that John presents a different perspective, a deified Jesus that goes beyond the human Jesus of the Synoptic Gospels and Old Testament Scriptures. However, when John's statements are read in their literary and cultural context, they fully align with the rest of the scriptural witness. He is not telling us anything different from what has been examined so far.

Trinitarians assume a divine person—"God the Son," who is incarnate in Jesus, is introduced in John's prologue and further expounded on in his Gospel text. However, this assumption needs to be challenged, because...

1. There is no precedence or grammatical necessity to capitalize the "Word" of John 1:1 or to view it as a preexistent, deified Jesus. For discussion about this, see Appendix A.

2. Other verses or passages used in John's Gospel to support a deified Jesus are also highly interpretive (and are likewise dealt with in Appendix A).

3. Throughout his Gospel, John makes it clear that it is the Father alive and at work in Jesus, which explains his inspired words, miraculous works, and clear revelation of God:

    • The Father is "the only true God" (17:3).
    • Jesus' works are the Father's works. These works were done by the Father (10:32; 10:37; 14:10; cf. Acts 2:22).
    • Jesus' words are the Father's words (8:48; 12:49-50; 14:10; cf. Deut. 18:18).
    • Jesus' glory is from the Father (1:14; 8:54; 17:5).
    • Jesus has declared or made known the Father (1:18; 14:10-11).
    • If people knew Jesus, they would know the Father (8:19; 12:45; 14:7-11).

4. Because Jesus spoke the Father's words and performed the Father's miraculous works, people could "know and understand that the Father is in me, and I in the Father" (10:38; see also John 12:49; 14:10).

5. Nothing in John's stated purpose for his Gospel would suggest

he is trying to portray Jesus as God:

> Jesus performed many other signs in the presence of his disciples, which are not recorded in this book. But these are written that you may believe that Jesus is the Messiah, the Son of God, and that by believing you may have life in his name (John 20:30-31).

6.   The statements of faith included in John's narrative do not present a deified Jesus:

> Then Nathanael declared, "Rabbi, you are the Son of God; you are the king of Israel." (1:49)

> "Yes, Lord," [Martha] replied, "I believe that you are the Messiah, the Son of God, who is to come into the world." (11:27)

Such statements of faith align with John's own, that "Jesus is the Messiah, the Son of God" (20:31).

7.   If John were seeking to portray Jesus as somehow beyond what the Synoptic Gospels declare of him, not only does he not make this intention clear, but he includes statements that positively work against it—statements that emphasize both Jesus' humanity and the supremacy of the Father over him:

> Yet a time is coming and has now come when the true worshipers will worship the Father in the Spirit and in truth, for they are the kind of worshipers the Father seeks. God is spirit, and his worshippers must worship in the Spirit and in truth. (4:23-24)

> Jesus gave them this answer: "Very truly I tell you, the Son can do nothing by himself; he can do only what he sees his Father doing, because whatever the Father does the Son also does." (5:19)

> By myself I can do nothing; I judge only as I hear, and my

judgment is just, for I seek not to please myself but him who
sent me. (5:30)

...you are looking for a way to kill me, a man who has told
you the truth that I heard from God. (8:40)

...for the Father is greater than I. (14:28)

Now this is eternal life: that they know you, the only true
God, and Jesus Christ, whom you have sent. (17:3)

Jesus said, "Do not hold on to me, for I have not yet ascended
to the Father. Go instead to my brothers and tell them, 'I
am ascending to my Father and your Father, to my God and
your God.'" (20:17)

With such statements, John stresses the humanity of Jesus even more
than the Synoptic Gospels. Fourteen times in John's Gospel, Jesus is
called a man (*anthropos*) without qualification (1:30; 4:29; 5:12; 7:46,
51; 8:40; 9:11, 16; 10:33; 11:47, 50; 18:14, 17, 29; 19:15), which is more
than all of the Synoptic Gospels combined. If John had Trinitarian
inclinations, it is highly unlikely that he would have been content
for these humanity statements about Jesus to remain unqualified
in some way.

THE ACTS OF THE APOSTLES

Key Point: In this historical account of the early church, there is no
evidence or indication that Christians held a deified view of Jesus—
or indeed, that they held any Christological belief that departed from
what is presented in the Gospels.

The view held by the apostles is declared by Peter on the
Day of Pentecost:

Fellow Israelites, listen to this: Jesus of Nazareth was a man
accredited by God to you by miracles, wonders and signs,
which God did among you through him, as you yourselves
know. This man was handed over to you by God's deliberate
plan and foreknowledge; and you, with the help of wicked

men, put him to death by nailing him to the cross. But God raised him from the dead, freeing him from the agony of death, because it was impossible for death to keep its hold on him...

God has raised this Jesus to life, and we are all witnesses of it. Exalted to the right hand of God, he has received from the Father the promised Holy Spirit and has poured out what you now see and hear. For David did not ascend to heaven, and yet he said, "The LORD said to my Lord: 'Sit at my right hand until I make your enemies a footstool for your feet.'" Therefore let all Israel be assured of this: God has made this Jesus, whom you crucified, both Lord and Messiah. (Acts 2:22-24, 32-36)

Some things to note:

- Twice, Peter says Jesus was a man—a human being—without qualification.
- The miracles, wonders, and signs performed by Jesus weren't done by his inherent powers, but by God at work "through him" (v. 22).
- It is God who raised Jesus from the dead. This is the consistent witness of Scripture—stated eight times in Acts, in addition to over 30 times elsewhere (e.g., Rom. 4:24; 6:4; 8:11; 10:9; 1 Cor. 6:14; 15:4, 15; 2 Cor. 4:14; 13:4; Gal. 1:1; Eph. 1:19-20; Col. 2:12; 1 Thess. 1:10; Heb. 13:20; 1 Pet. 1:21). Further, there are 28 occasions when the divine passive is used to signify that Jesus "was raised" by God. The Bible never teaches that Jesus raised himself.[2] How could he, being dead?
- The Messiah, and what happened to him, were all part of

2. Some quote Jesus' statements in John 2:19; 10:17-18 as exceptions expressing that Jesus raised himself. However, closer examination of the context and use of the divine passive shows that they align with the consistent New Testament teaching that it was the Father who raised Jesus.

God's "deliberate plan and foreknowledge" (v. 23).

- The resurrected Jesus is now ascended and glorified at God's right hand.
- The Holy Spirit, Jesus' glorification, his victory, authority, and kingdom rule, his lordship as Messiah, were all given to him from the Father.
- Jesus is declared to be "Lord and Messiah" (v. 36). Throughout Acts, the gospel declarations do not include belief in a deified Jesus as a requisite for salvation: "they never stopped teaching and proclaiming the good news that Jesus is the Messiah" (Acts 5:42).

Subsequent proclamations confirm the above: Jesus is the servant of "the God of Abraham, Isaac and Jacob" (Acts 3:13), "the God of our ancestors" (Acts 5:30). He is the one whom *Yahweh* has resurrected and glorified (Acts 3:26), and through whom alone salvation is possible (Acts 4:12). In all 15 declarations of the gospel recorded in Acts, the message accords with what Paul says:

> I am saying nothing beyond what the prophets and Moses said would happen—that the Messiah would suffer and, as the first to rise from the dead, would bring the message of light to his own people and to the Gentiles. (Acts 26:22-23)

If the apostles taught the deity of Christ or a different understanding of God, it would have been inexplicable for such ground-breaking and earth-shattering doctrine at the time, not to appear in the history of the early church in the book of Acts.

The Letters of the Apostle Paul

Key Point: Paul has a high and exalted view of Jesus Christ, but is always careful to place him in a different category from and subordinate position to his Father God.

Paul expresses very clearly and concisely his understanding *and this differentiation*, when he says:

> "There is no God but one." For even if there are so-called

gods, whether in heaven or on earth (as indeed there are many "gods" and many "lords"), yet for us there is but one God, the Father, from whom all things came and for whom we live; and there is but one Lord, Jesus Christ, through whom all things came and through whom we live. (1 Cor. 8:4-6)

Paul comments on the multiplicity of belief and fluidity in meaning around those identified as gods or lords in the culture of his day, which we have already noted. "Yet for us"—that is, for Christians—we believe in only one God, who Paul identifies and defines as the Father (not a Trinity), and one Lord, who is the Messiah, Jesus.

To further emphasize the distinction, he notes that the Father is the source and originator of all things (Greek: *Ek* "out of"), the creator and the fulfiller (*eis*) of the world and human beings. In contrast, Jesus is the means or mediator "through whom" (*dia*) these things have come to be. This aligns with Paul's "Wisdom Christology" in this letter, where Jesus is seen as "the wisdom of God" (1 Cor. 1:24). Just as God created the world through Wisdom (Prov. 8:22-31), so God has brought all things (Greek: *ta panta*) into being through Christ (2 Cor 5:17-18).[3]

Throughout Paul's writings, the focus is not on God's original creation, but his new creation (2 Cor. 3:6; 5:7). By virtue of Christ's now exalted position, a new spiritual world order has been ushered in, whereby all other gods and lords, all other principalities and powers, are subject to Christ Jesus, God's sovereign king (Acts 2:33-35; Eph. 1:22; Col. 1:17-30). He is the one in and through whom we live (John 14:6; 20:31; Gal. 2:20).

It is important to note that Paul is consistent in his terminology throughout his writings, a few disputed verses (addressed in

---

3. Paul uses this term for "all things" much more broadly than just the original or physical creation. See Charles H. Welch, "All and All Things," Heaven Dwellers, accessed April 14, 2021, http://www.heavendwellers.com/hd_aa_all_and_all_things.htm.

Appendix A) and a few quotes from the LXX notwithstanding.[4] When Paul refers to the Lord in his letters (over 200 times), he is speaking of the Lord Messiah, the Lord Jesus, not the Lord God. When he says "God" he is always speaking of the Father. He does not confuse the two.

For example: "There is...one Lord, one faith, one baptism; one God and Father of all, who is over all and through all and in all" (Eph. 4:4-6). Here the one "Lord" Jesus is set apart from the one supreme and almighty "God and Father."

Moreover, when Paul talks of there being only one God (Rom. 3:30; 16:27; Gal. 3:20; 1 Tim. 1:17, 25) it is clear he is referring to God the Father (Eph. 1:3, 17; 5:20; Phil. 4:20; 1 Thess. 1:9; 5:23, etc.) and is not including Jesus. The Father is the only wise, eternal, true and living God, immortal, whom nobody has seen (1 Tim. 6:13-16; Rom. 16:27; 1 Thess. 1:9)—the one from whom, through whom and to whom are all things (Rom. 11:36). Paul constantly declares that he is the "God and Father of our Lord Jesus Christ" (Rom. 15:6; 2 Cor. 1:3; Eph. 1:3; see also 2 Cor. 11:31; Col. 1:3; Gal. 1:4, etc.). Paul's clear, consistent, and overwhelming testimony is not that Jesus is God, but that he has a God, who is the Father.

There is also an absolute consistency within Paul's writings that God the Father is the author, originator, or "first cause" in the universe. This is denoted by the Greek preposition *ek,* "from, out of" which is used of God, but never of Jesus. All things are from God (Rom. 11:36; 1 Cor. 8:6; 11:12; 2 Cor. 5:18). This is also expressed in the epistles in other ways: God "created all things" (Eph. 3:9), is the "builder of everything" (Heb. 3:4), "gives life to everything" (1 Tim. 6:13), and is the one "through whom everything exists" (Heb. 2:10).

Paul's doctrine aligns with the rest of the scriptural witness that God the Father (*Yahweh*) alone is the ultimate source of everything

---

4. An example is Romans 10:13. By the way, some Trinitarians argue that because Old Testament texts that originally referred to *Yahweh* are applied to Jesus in the New Testament, as here, this indicates the authors saw Jesus as God. This is logically and exegetically invalid — see "the Bible teaches that David is God," by Dale Tuggy, *Trinities*, November 6, 2019, https://trinities.org/blog/the-bible-teaches-that-david-is-god/.

(e.g., Isa. 44:24; John 11:4; Acts 5:12). Paul's overwhelming references to God's purposes "in Christ" or "in the Lord," "through Christ" and "for Christ" express his understanding that Jesus is God's mediator, means, intention, and goal within God's redemptive plan: his re-creation and emerging new world order.

Paul is also consistent in his understanding that Jesus' status is below that of the Father. Just as "the head of every man is Christ...the head of Christ is God" (1 Cor. 11:3).

> For [God] "has put everything under [Christ's] feet." Now when it says that "everything" has been put under him, it is clear that this does not include God himself, who put everything under Christ. When he has done this, then the Son himself will be made subject to him who put everything under him, so that God may be all in all. (1 Cor. 15:27-28)

Note that here, the context is the future consummation of this age and ushering in of the age to come. It is not, as some Trinitarians claim, that Jesus was subject to the Father only for a season during his incarnation as a man; it is also true of his present glorified position and future status.

Make no mistake, Paul connects and aligns Jesus in the strongest terms with his Father. It is not that Jesus is God, but that he is "of God" (1 Cor. 3:23), and "the image of God" (2 Cor. 4:4; see also Col. 1:15). "God was pleased to have all his fullness dwell in him" (Col. 1:19), "for in Christ all the fullness of the Deity lives in bodily form" (Col. 2:9). This reminds us of Jesus' words: "I and the Father are one" (John 10:30), and "Anyone who has seen me has seen the Father" (John 14:9). "The Son is the radiance of God's glory and the exact representation of his being" (Heb. 1:3).

To say that Jesus is God's image is to indicate very strongly that he is separate in being from his Father. In principle, nothing can be the "image" of itself: they are necessarily two separate entities. My image as reflected in a mirror or captured in a photograph portrays and reveals clearly what I am like, but *is not me*. I may show somebody my photo and say, "This is me," but I mean it representatively, not ontologically. My comment is similar to Jesus saying of the bread, "This is my body." The bread is not the same as Jesus' body, it *represents* his body.

Paul sees Jesus and the Father, Christ and God, as one in character, spirit, and purpose. But he never crosses the line of making Jesus and God one in status or essence. Jesus is the dearly loved son of God (Col. 1:13), who is exalted at his right hand (Col. 3:1) and to whom God has subjected all things (Eph. 1:20-22).

Moreover, Paul sees Jesus as a man who was "born (literally in the Greek text: "came into existence") of a woman" (Gal. 4:4). In Paul's Christology, Jesus is the second "Adam," or representative man, patterned after the first human being (Rom. 5:14). Through Jesus' willing submission and obedience to God on the cross, he overcame the consequences of the disobedience of the first Adam:

> But the gift is not like the trespass. For if the many died by the trespass of the one man, how much more did God's grace and the gift that came by the grace of the one man, Jesus Christ, overflow to the many! (Rom. 5:15; cf. 1 Cor. 15:47-49)

Paul's clear statement in 1 Timothy 2:5 summarizes the above: "For there is one God and one mediator between God and mankind, the man Christ Jesus."

Throughout Paul's writings, there is no indication that he departed in any way from the Old Testament Scriptures (Acts 26:27) or the Gospel testimonies about Jesus. There are a few disputed passages where Trinitarians contend differently. These are discussed in Appendix A.

Other Epistles

Hebrews

Whether it was Paul or another author who penned this book, their Christology is completely consistent. The author's intent is to portray the superiority of the Messiah and the New Covenant over the old Jewish dispensation. In the introduction, the author clearly presents Christ's exalted position as God's son and heir—above the angels but under the Father. There is some translation bias and contested interpretation in this epistle's introduction, considered in Appendix A.

JAMES

Nothing in James' letter would suggest his theology is different from the rest of the New Testament writings on the nature of God and Christ. There is "one God" (2:19), "our Father" (1:27), who is unchanging, from whom all good things come (1:17) and who cannot be tempted (1:13). He is seen as distinct from "our glorious Lord Jesus Christ" (2:1).

PETER

In his introduction, Peter echoes Paul's repeated salutations when he says, "Praise be to the God and Father of our Lord Jesus Christ" (1 Pet. 1:3). He goes on to affirm: "Through [Christ] you believe in God, who raised him from the dead and glorified him, and so your faith and hope are in God" (1:21). Believers "revere Christ as Lord" (3:15), for he has suffered "to bring [us] to God" (3:18) and "has gone into heaven and is at God's right hand—with angels, authorities and powers in submission to him" (3:22). This aligns with and echoes Pauline Christology.

Peter delivers seven speeches in the book of Acts (2:14-40; 3:12-26; 4:8-12; 5:29-32; 10:34-43; 11:5-17; 15:7-29)—a total of 97 verses—in which he speaks of the one God of the patriarchs (3:13, 25; 5:30), who anointed and empowered (2:22; 10:38) his servant Jesus (3:13, 26), a man (2:22), whom God raised from the dead (2:24; 3:15, 26; 4:10; 5:30; 10:40) and exalted as "Lord and Messiah" (2:36; see also 10:36) at his right hand in heaven (5:31). Jesus is "Prince and Savior" (5:31), the only one through whom we can be saved (4:12). Peter's theology and Christology in both his speeches in Acts and his letters harmonize beautifully.

John

In John's Gospel, he expresses his purpose: "that you may believe that Jesus is the Messiah, the Son of God, and that by believing you may have life in his name" (John 20:31). His letters expand further, but do not depart from these fundamentals of belief. God the Father is "light" (1 John 1:5) and "love" (1 John 4:8, 16), "whom no one has seen" (1 John 4:12). He is "the true God" (1 John 5:20). Jesus Christ is God's one and only son (1 John 3:8; 4:15; 5:10-12) whom he sent into the world (4:9, 14). He is the holy one who laid down his life for us (3:16), the "Righteous One" who is our advocate (2:1) and our Savior, through whom we have life (5:12).

It's interesting that John makes the strong statement that "no one has ever seen God" (1 John 4:12), yet he begins his New Testament epistle with these words:

> That which was from the beginning, which we have heard, which we have seen with our eyes, which we have looked at and our hands have touched—this we proclaim concerning the Word of life. (1 John 1:1)

John is asserting most strongly that he has seen Jesus, yet he has not seen God. If John believed Jesus to be God, this would make no sense.

Even though some translations capitalize "Word," as here in the NIV, four times in this introductory statement John says that this word is a "what," not a "who" (Greek ό, not ός)—it is something, not someone. This "word of life" is God's promised plan and purpose for his people, delivered to us through his son. Some scholars believe that John may have been taking pains to correct misunderstandings that were already beginning to arise concerning his Gospel prologue (John 1:1).

As he concludes his letter, John makes it abundantly clear that "the true God" doesn't include Jesus, but is the Father. Rather, Jesus "has come and has given us understanding, so that we may know him who is true...the true God" (1 John 5:20).

Moreover, John focuses on the outworking of our faith in obedience and love as a test of its authenticity, and states among his non-negotiables "that Jesus Christ has come in the flesh" (1 John 4:2-3). Many believe these emphases are a direct rebuttal of Gnostic heresy that was already beginning to take believers captive. This will be looked at further in the next chapter.

JUDE

This short letter upholds the same understanding of God and Jesus observed so far throughout. The "only God" (v. 25) is "God the Father" (v. 1). The "only Sovereign and Lord" (v. 4) is Jesus Christ (vv. 1, 4), and the two are seen as quite distinct (vv. 20, 25).

REVELATION

The introduction makes it clear that this revelation did not originate from Jesus himself, but was given to him from God for him to pass on. If Jesus were fully God and all-knowing, why would this be necessary?

From the outset, there is a clear distinction of persons, and throughout, this differentiation is maintained. The Lord God Almighty is introduced and referred to in terms unique to this book: "who is, and who was, and who is to come" (1:4, 8; see also 4:8; 11:17; 16:5). This is generally understood as an expression of God's timelessness and an interpretation of his name, *YHWH* (Exod. 3:14; Ps. 90:2; Isa. 41:4, 16; 43:10; 48:12). It is not applied to Jesus, but is unique to the Father.

Jesus Christ is introduced as "the faithful witness, the firstborn from the dead, and the ruler of the kings of the earth" (Rev. 1:5), which echoes the affirmations in Philippians 2, Colossians 1, and Hebrews 1-2. "We do not yet see everything in subjection to him" (Heb. 2:8, ESV), but his full position of authority and power will be realized when he comes with the clouds (Rev. 1:7; Matt. 23:39; 24:31) and is universally acknowledged as Lord, with ultimate authority under God.

Jesus is the one "who loves us and has freed us from our sins by his blood, and has made us to be a kingdom and priests to serve his God and Father" (1:5-6). Notice here that the Father is referenced as Jesus' God, as elsewhere in the book, by Jesus himself:

The one who is victorious I will make a pillar in the temple of
my God. Never again will they leave it. I will write on them
the name of *my* God and the name of the city of *my* God,
the new Jerusalem, which is coming down out of heaven
from *my* God; and I will also write on them my new name.
(3:12; emphasis added)

Consistently throughout the New Testament (John 17:3;
20:17; 1 Cor. 15:24-28, etc.), as here in the book of Revelation, the
superior position of God over Jesus is always acknowledged.

The description of John's vision of Jesus (1:9-20), subsequently
affirmed in the messages to the seven churches, portrays a glorified "Son
of Man" similar to Jesus' appearance on the Mount of Transfiguration
(Luke 9:29) and in Daniel's vision (Dan. 7:9-10). As "the image of the
invisible God" (Col. 1:15) he reflects his Father's glory and qualities,
as Eric Chang notes:

It is more in line with scriptural teaching to say that God has
conferred on Christ some of his divine titles and attributes.
Christ acts as the Father's plenipotentiary, such that when
he speaks, it is God who speaks through him; when he does
something, it is the Almighty who works in him; when he
comes in the name of his Father, the Lord God comes in him
(Rev. 22:12-13).[5]

Throughout Revelation, all anthems of praise and adoration are
directed to the Lord God Almighty for who he is and what he has done
(4:8-11; 11:17; 14:7; 15:3-4; 16:5-7; 19:1-8; 21:23). In chapter 5, the
focus is on the Lamb, with honor given to him. Because he was "slain"
(vv. 9, 12), and for his redemption of mankind (vv. 9-10), he is worthy
to open the scrolls and to "receive power and wealth and wisdom and
strength and honor and glory and praise" (v. 12). Worship is expressed
to both God and the Lamb in verse 13, as any honor given to Jesus is
ultimately to God's glory (John 17:1; Phil. 2:11).

---

5. Eric H. H. Chang, *The Only Perfect Man: The Glory of God in the Face of Jesus
Christ*, 2nd ed., ed. Bentley Chan, (Charleston, SC: Christian Disciples Church, 2017), 197.

There is no question that Jesus is worthy of our praise and adoration as Lord and Savior, but not as Almighty God. Even in Jesus' glorification, the distinction is made between God, who throughout Revelation is "on the throne" (4:9; 5:1, 7, 13; 6:16; 7:15; 20:11; 21:5), and Jesus, who is at his right hand or before the throne (5:6-14).[6]

Summary:

This overview points to the consistency of the biblical witness to the one and only almighty, personal God named *Yahweh*, and his anointed, unique, and deeply cherished son, Jesus. This begotten son of God is the Messiah, who through the power of the Holy Spirit, fully and clearly revealed his Father's character and lived out his will.

He was conceived supernaturally and born of a woman as a human being. He was sent by God to take away the sin of the world through his sacrificial death on the cross, was raised from death by the Father and is now glorified at God's right hand above all others as supreme Lord, head of the church, and our High Priest who mediates for us. One day he will return in power and glory to judge the world, restore all things, and establish God's eternal kingdom.

---

6. Many Trinitarians believe that because Jesus is worshiped, he must be God. But this misconception is not supported, either logically or theologically. See "Podcast 21: Should We Worship Jesus?," by Sean Finnegan, *Restitutio*, March 4, 2016, https://restitutio. org/2016/03/04/should-we-worship-jesus/; Dr. Dale Tuggy, "Who Should Christians Worship? Part 1," State University of New York at Fredonia, May 22, 2012, video of lecture, https://www.youtube.com/watch?v=9IPJq1kcDuc&ab_channel=khanpadawan.

CHAPTER 6

WHO IS JESUS?

MANY CHRISTIANS HAVE A "Superman" view of Jesus. This superhero character came to earth in a space capsule from the planet Krypton and was raised by Jonathan and Martha Kent, who named him Clark. Clark Kent resides in the fictional American city of Metropolis, where he works as a journalist for the Daily Planet newspaper. Although he looks no different from normal people, Clark possesses innate superpowers by virtue of his unique origin, which he employs when needed to fight crime and evil in the world. He protects his identity by swapping into his iconic red and blue caped costume when he performs his superhuman feats.

In a similar way, many Christians see Jesus as preexistent in another place (heaven) before coming to earth. Even though he was raised by human parents and looked like everyone else, they think, he had a secret identity and possessed inherent special powers by virtue of his non-human nature and non-earthly origin. He would employ these powers at times when the situation demanded.

Other Christians have a "demigod" view of Jesus. Demigods were prevalent in Greek and Roman culture before and after the time of Christ. Simply put, a demigod is a human of such heroic or special nature that he or she is seen as being partly divine. Sometimes this special status was the result of the sexual union between a deity and a human, or because of some unique quality or power the individual possessed, or some superhuman feat they had performed.

In Greek mythology, the demigods generally existed in a separate realm from that of mere mortals; but they could also enter human society (e.g., Acts 14:11-13; 28:6). Most of the Roman emperors of the first three centuries after Christ claimed divinity by virtue of their exalted position and power. Similarly, Jesus is seen by many in this demigod category. He is a mix of the mortal and the immortal, of the natural and the supernatural, of the human and the divine, simultaneously both God and man.

As we've seen, such perceptions of Jesus naturally arise out of Trinitarian doctrine, which, since the fourth century, has become the orthodox theological position of the institutional church and is now deeply ingrained and entrenched in modern Christianity's beliefs and culture.

After the deconstruction of the previous chapters, it's time to engage in some reconstruction. If the biblical Jesus is different from the Trinitarian Jesus, how then should we perceive and understand him? I offer the following as a start:

1. Jesus is a Man (but not just any man)

Hear me out... I am not saying that he is JUST a man. He is infinitely more than that. But he is a human being. If Jesus personally preexisted his conception, he can't be a normal person. If Jesus shares, or has shared in, the supernatural attributes of God, then he can't also be truly human.[1] If Jesus is fully God, he can't also be fully man.

I believe that, unfortunately, Jesus' humanity has often been confused, complicated, or compromised by his supposed deity, diminishing the raw reality of how he truly lived as a man of God in faith and total reliance upon his Heavenly Father.

In the Chalcedonian Creed (AD 451), Trinitarians sought to address the confusion around what was seen as the union of God and man in Jesus, and some heretical views that had arisen about it. Notwithstanding their philosophical speculation and semantics around Jesus being simultaneously and completely two natures, their theological conception boiled down to Jesus being in essence God, with the human part an "add-on" at his birth—his incarnation.

---

1. Dale Tuggy and Christopher M. Date, *Is Jesus Human and Not Divine?* (Warrendale, PA: Areopagus Books, 2020), ch. 1.

The New Testament writers don't seem to share any such reluctance concerning Jesus' humanity. They state clearly that Jesus was "a man"—fully human—and constantly attest to this being the case. They declare that he was "born of a woman" (Gal. 4:4), an expression that means he was fully human and mortal (Job 14:1; 15:14; 25:4; 1 Cor. 11:12; Luke 7:28). They acknowledge that he was a natural descendant of Adam and Eve (Luke 3:38), Abraham (Gal. 3:16), and David (2 Tim. 2:8).

> Jesus is the physical descendant—miraculously generated by the Spirit of God in Mary—of the biological chain from the ancestry of Jewish men and women—summarized in the twin descriptions, "the seed of the woman" and the "son of David."[2]

Peter declared on the Day of Pentecost: "Fellow Israelites, listen to this: Jesus of Nazareth was a man..." (Acts 2:22). Paul makes it clear when he says: "For there is one God and one mediator between God and mankind, the man Christ Jesus" (1 Tim. 2:5).

Actually the Greek text here is more literally "a man" or "a human." In Galatians 4:4, Paul says, "But when the set time had fully come, God sent his Son, born of a woman, born under the law." Although most translations render the Greek *genomenon* here as "born" it literally means "came into existence." The Gospel writers use the same Greek root word when they attest that Jesus' existence began at his physical birth (Matt. 1:1, 18). This was literally his beginning (*genesis*).

John also makes this clear. In his first letter he states clearly three essentials of belief:

- Jesus is the "Christ" (or Messiah) the "Son of God" (1 John 2:22-23; 5:1, 5).
- Only through the Son can we share in eternal life (1 John 5:11-12).

---

2. Greg S. Deuble, *They Never Told Me This in Church,* 2nd ed. (Fayetteville, GA: Restoration Fellowship, 2010), 172.

- Jesus Christ has come (literally) "in flesh": "This is how you can recognize the Spirit of God: Every spirit that acknowledges that Jesus Christ has come in the flesh is from God, but every spirit that does not acknowledge Jesus is not from God. This is the spirit of the antichrist, which you have heard is coming and even now is already in the world" (1 John 4:2-3).

John then reiterates this in his second letter:

> I say this because many deceivers, who do not acknowledge Jesus Christ as coming in the flesh, have gone out into the world. Any such person is the deceiver and the antichrist. (2 John 7)

Why did John so strongly add this third nonnegotiable to the other two that were in his Gospel (John 20:31)? Many believe that it was because by the end of the first century, Greek philosophical thinking had already begun to infiltrate the church: "I am writing these things to you about those who are trying to lead you astray" (1 John 2:26). Paul had warned against it: "See to it that no one takes you captive through hollow and deceptive philosophy" (Col. 2:8). Aspects of Gnosticism seemed to be already taking a foothold in some Christian communities, and needed to be addressed, as seen in Paul's admonitions to the Colossians (Col. 2:20-23) and the Corinthians (1 Cor. 6:12-20).

Gnostic philosophy was prominent in the Greco-Roman world at the time. It was built on Platonic dualism, which separated the conceptual, intellectual world from the earthly, material world. The conceptual world was ideal, spiritual and inherently good, whereas the material world was a corruption, or imperfect version, and therefore inherently ignorant or evil. Gnosticism had various iterations—some positing that because the body was evil, physical desires needed to be subjugated (Col. 2:20-23). Others believed these physical urges were insignificant and could be indulged (1 Cor. 6:12-20).

What is relevant to our discussion is that a belief was beginning to emerge that if the physical is corrupt, then Christ's body was also corrupt. Some found it impossible to understand how God could bring about ultimate and consummate good through a natural man with a physical body.

This led to the "Docetic heresy": that Jesus only *appeared* to have a human body. The Christ "spirit" must have entered into his body at some point (perhaps at his baptism) and departed or withdrawn subsequently (perhaps on the cross). Jesus' bodily resurrection was either dismissed or seen as spiritual and metaphysical rather than physical and actual. His resurrection was typically spurned by the Greek philosophers: "When they heard about the resurrection of the dead, some of them sneered..." (Acts 17:32).

With this background, you can understand why John is so strong in his statements about Jesus being fully human and having come as a man "in flesh." Some perceive this same Gnostic philosophical influence within the subsequent formulation of the doctrine of the Trinity. Within Trinitarianism, there was and still is a hesitancy to see Jesus as a finite man—completely human. However, there isn't any teaching in the Bible about Jesus having a composite nature, a supposed mixture of deity and humanity. The Bible teaches he is a man: totally human.

The scriptural witness to Jesus being fully human is further demonstrated in that...

- The Hebrew term "Son of Man" is also understood as simply "man" (e.g., Num. 23:19; Ps. 8:4).
- This title, "Son of Man," is Jesus' preferred self-designation. It appears 82 times in the Gospels—in the Synoptics almost exclusively, where he also never calls himself "Son of God." In John's Gospel, "Son of Man" appears 13 times.
- God "alone is immortal" (1 Tim. 6:16), whereas Jesus died. Jesus has been granted immortality by the Father (John 5:26; 6:57) as we will be (1 Cor. 15:53-54), but only God is eternally and essentially immortal. He cannot die, has never died, and will not die.
- No one "has seen or can see" God (1 Tim. 6:15-16), but Jesus was physically visible and observed. That's why he is

"the image of the invisible God" (Col. 1:15): a reflection of God, not himself God.

- God is complete in himself, and the source of "every good and perfect gift" (James 1:17). There is nothing we have that we didn't receive from him (1 Cor. 4:7). Likewise, there is no statement in the Bible that suggests Jesus possesses something he did not, or has not, received from his Father (Matt. 11:27; 28:18; Luke 22:29; Eph. 1:20-23). "Now they know that everything you have given me comes from you" (John 17:7).

2. Jesus is a Unique Man

Jesus is unique. The Greek word *monogenes* in John 1:14, 3:16, 18, and 1 John 4:9 means he is "one of a kind—the only one in his category." He is...

UNIQUELY CHOSEN

Here is my servant whom I have chosen
The one I love, in whom I delight;
I will put my Spirit on him,
And he will proclaim justice to the nations... (Matt 12:18; see also Isa. 42:1)

He was chosen before the creation of the world, but was revealed in these last times for your sake. (1 Pet. 1:20)

From the very beginning, God had in mind the one who would be an "offspring" of Eve (Gen. 3:15), through whom he would restore the world and bring it to its intended culmination. As the Messiah, Jesus is the ultimate chosen one.

UNIQUELY CONCEIVED AND BEGOTTEN

Jesus was begotten. Not "eternally begotten" (whatever that means) as expressed in the creeds, but begotten historically, at a point in time—

"today" or this day (Ps. 2:7; Heb. 1:5).

Just as the first man, Adam, was specially created, so Jesus was also specially procreated—conceived by the Holy Spirit in Mary. The explanation given by the angel to her was, "The Holy Spirit will come on you, and the power of the Most High will overshadow you. So the holy one to be born will be called the Son of God" (Luke 1:35).

Uniquely Loved

Jesus is God's unique son (John 1:14; 3:16). As we've seen, the term "Son of God" in Scripture is not an ontological term. It's a relational term. As sons or children of God we have been adopted into his family and share in a loving relationship with our brother Jesus and our Heavenly Father.

But as God's unique son, Jesus is the apple of God's eye—"the One [God] loves" (Eph 1:6). He has a special place in the Father's heart, as God expressed openly on more than one occasion: "You are my Son, whom I love; with you I am well pleased" (Luke 3:22; see also Matt. 17:5).

Love for God is expressed in obedience, faith, and surrender to his will (John 15:10; 1 John 2:15-17). Nobody has loved God to nearly the degree that Jesus has. Hence, he has a special status in relationship with the Father by virtue of his unique birth, sinless life, total love and submission, sacrificial death, and subsequent glorification and reward.

Uniquely Called and Sent

Jesus was specially tasked for his saving work in God's redemptive plan. His birth announcement declared this: "Today in the town of David a Savior has been born to you; he is the Messiah, the Lord" (Luke 2:11). Jesus is "the Lamb of God, who takes away the sin of the world" (John 1:29). For this we will be forever grateful and he will be eternally praised (Rev. 1:6; 5:12).

Uniquely Anointed and Empowered

Messiah means "anointed one." Jesus was the one specially set apart, commissioned, authorized, and empowered to fulfill God's mission in, to, and for the world. We see this anointing and commissioning expressed at his baptism, with the words of God's approval and the visible outpouring of the Spirit upon him (Matt. 3:16-17; Mark 1:9-11; Luke 3:21-22; Acts 10:38, 42). "The Father loves the Son and has placed everything in his hands" (John 3:35).

In order for Jesus to "[speak] the words of God" and do what the Father entrusted to him, God gave to Jesus "the Spirit without limit" (John 3:34). God's Spirit was at work in Christ, unhindered and without restriction, enabling him to be and do all that God had called him to be and do.

Uniquely Glorified

> Therefore God exalted him to the highest place and gave him the name that is above every name, that at the name of Jesus every knee should bow, in heaven and on earth and under the earth, and every tongue acknowledge that Jesus Christ is Lord, to the glory of God the Father. (Phil. 2:9-11)

> [God] raised Christ from the dead and seated him at his right hand in the heavenly realms, far above all rule and authority, power and dominion, and every name that is invoked, not only in the present age but also in the one to come. And God placed all things under his feet and appointed him to be head over everything for the church, which is his body, the fullness of him who fills everything in every way. (Eph. 1:20-23)

Jesus is literally God's anointed right hand man (Ps. 80:17), to whom God has subjected everything and everyone else. He stands second only to the one who is "all in all" within the cosmos—*Yahweh* himself:

> For he [i.e. God the Father] "has put everything under his [i.e. Jesus'] feet." Now when it says that "everything" has been put under him, it is clear that this does not include God himself, who put everything under Christ. When he has done this, then the Son himself will be made subject to him

who put everything under him, so that God may be all in all.
(1 Cor. 15:27-28)

3. Jesus is the Perfected Man

TOTALLY SURRENDERED

When I was a Trinitarian, the following passage was among many I found problematic:

> During the days of Jesus' life on earth, he offered up prayers
> and petitions with fervent cries and tears to the one who
> could save him from death, and he was heard because of
> his reverent submission. Son though he was, he learned
> obedience from what he suffered and, once made perfect,
> he became the source of eternal salvation for all who obey
> him... (Heb. 5:7-10)

We see here that Jesus was "made perfect," not that he was intrinsically or already perfect (v. 9). His perfection, or completion in maturity, was the result of ongoing "reverent submission" and "learned obedience" through the crucible of suffering (vv. 7-8).

Notice that this earnest supplication and fervent petition was an ongoing process: "during the days" (plural) of his life on earth (v. 7). We can see specific examples in the wilderness and Gethsemane, but it appears there was an ongoing crying out to the Father for a submissive and obedient spirit in the midst of constant temptation and challenges throughout his life and ministry. As Jesus called on his disciples to do, he himself took up his cross daily in ongoing self-surrender.

If Jesus was fully God, and God cannot be tempted (James 1:13), how do we understand and explain his earthly temptations? Was this a mere parody? Play acting? Was it the "human" part of Jesus being tempted? And if so, what was his "god" part doing at the time?

The culminating challenge to Jesus' total surrender and obedience to the Father seems to be in the garden of Gethsemane before his arrest. It's been said that on the cross Jesus died for us, but in Gethsemane he died to himself. It may be in this spiritual sense that the writer to the Hebrews is expressing it—that the Father was the one who could save Jesus, not just from physical death, but primarily from a spiritual "death" of disobedience and lack of surrender, as happened to Adam.

Jesus' struggle in the garden was for him to submit to the Father's will when everything within him was screaming out, "I don't want to do this!" That titanic battle was won through cries and tears and fervent prayer: "...he prayed more earnestly, and his sweat was like drops of blood falling to the ground" (Luke 22:44). We see here two distinct wills, with Jesus' ultimate submission to his Father: "...yet not my will, but yours be done" (v. 42). How can there be two distinct wills, one struggling to align with the other, if Jesus and his Father are supposedly ontologically one being?

The reality, enormity, wonder, and grandeur of Jesus' victory over temptation and sin is not possible in Trinitarian theology. In fact, it's not even tenable if the two are totally one, sharing the same essence, with Jesus possessing a divine, perfect, completely mature will, identical to the Father.

> In bringing many sons and daughters to glory, it was fitting that God, for whom and through whom everything exists, should make the pioneer of their salvation perfect through what he suffered. (Heb. 2:10)

"FAITH-FULL"

The spiritual principle that "the righteous will live by faith" (Rom. 1:17), is no less true of the righteous one, the trail-blazer of our faith:

> ...fixing our eyes on Jesus, the pioneer and perfecter of faith. For the joy set before him he endured the cross, scorning its shame, and sat down at the right hand of the throne of God. (Heb. 12:2)

In evangelical circles we focus almost exclusively on "faith *in* Jesus," but the Scriptures also talk about the "faith *of* Jesus." In fact, many well known texts (e.g., Rom. 3:22, 26; Gal. 2:16, 20; Phil. 3:9) that are often translated as "faith in" Christ can just as correctly be translated as the "faith of" Christ (subjective genitive, as opposed to objective genitive in Greek). This puts a whole different perspective on what constitutes saving faith, as well as what God is calling us to in terms of our response to the gospel.

For the Jews, to hear was to obey (Deut. 6:3-4; Mark 4:23; Luke 14:35; Rom. 11:8; Rev. 2:17). They understood faith as a whole-life commitment, an ongoing allegiance. The later influence of Greek philosophy focused on faith as intellectual assent—believing certain facts or accepting orthodox tenets of doctrine. But the biblical faith that justifies (Rom. 3:28; Gal. 2:16; 3:11, 24) is both faith *in* Jesus and the faith *of* Jesus. It is both a life-changing choice and a life-transforming process. It defines the path we are on and the progress we are making. It's not just about a decision, but about discipleship—following Jesus, which includes emulating his faith in his Father.

Jesus' whole life was a demonstration of faith. His public ministry began with his commissioning—the Spirit's anointing and God's declaration that Jesus was indeed his son, the Messiah. Immediately after, Jesus was challenged to live by faith in the messianic prophecies and promises of the Old Testament (e.g., Pss. 2, 110:1; Dan. 7). In the wilderness, Satan tempted him to misuse his position and authority— to serve himself or to bypass God's intended path of suffering (Luke 4:1-13). But Jesus chose instead to obey God's will and trust in his word: "it is written" (Luke 4:4, 8). Between the bookends of his ministry—the wilderness temptations and Gethsemane's struggle— there was an ongoing choice to live his life fully in alignment and submission to his Father's will.

Jesus was able to live as he did, teach what he taught, and accomplish all he achieved, not in his own strength, or because as God he had inherent supernatural powers that we mere mortals don't have.

It was because he fully depended on his Father, relying on the Holy Spirit at work in and through him. Jesus made this abundantly clear:

- "...the Son can do nothing by himself; he can only do what he sees his Father doing..." (John 5:19).
- "By myself I can do nothing" (John 5:30).
- "These words you hear are not my own; they belong to the Father who sent me" (John 14:24).

The Bible teaches that faith is needed and exercised in the absence of sight or proof: "Now faith is confidence in what we hope for and assurance about what we do not see" (Heb. 11:1); "We fix our eyes not on what is seen, but on what is unseen" and "we live by faith, not by sight" (2 Cor. 4:18; 5:7).

If, as Trinitarians claim, Jesus was consciously with the Father from eternity past and was himself God, then he didn't need faith, for he had already seen. Nor did he need hope in his adoption to sonship, as we are called to exercise: "...hope that is seen is no hope at all. Who hopes for what they already have?" (Rom. 8:24).

Jesus can hardly be our model to imitate, our example in faith, hope, and Christian living (1 Cor. 11:1; Heb. 12:3), if he is essentially different from us. How can we "follow in his steps" (1 Pet. 2:21) and "live as Jesus did" (1 John 2:6), when he had prior experiences, innate insight, special knowledge, miraculous powers, and divine attributes that we cannot access?[3]

And of course, it works in reverse: how could Jesus really understand and identify with us if he did not fully experience our human condition in all its challenges, limitations, and temptations? Thank God, our Savior and great High Priest is one with whom we can fully identify, and one who can completely empathize with us:

For we do not have a high priest who is unable to empathize

---

3. For further discussion on Jesus' faith, see "Podcast 146 - Jesus as an Exemplar of Faith in the New Testament," by Dale Tuggy, *Trinities*, July 11, 2016, https://trinities.org/blog/podcast-146-jesus-exemplar-faith-new-testament/.

with our weaknesses, but we have one who has been tempted in every way, just as we are—yet he did not sin. (Heb. 4:15)

THE REPRESENTATIVE MAN

From the beginning, God's intention for man was that we be in his image and likeness (Gen. 1:26), that we have dominion in the world (1:26, 28), and that we be blessed with abundant life (1:28; 2:9) as we work with God (2:15, 9-20) and walk with God (3:8) in intimate communion.

Unfortunately, the first Adam's disobedience disrupted God's loving plan and good intentions for us. But the second Adam's obedience has restored what was lost (1 Cor. 15:45-49). Jesus has made it possible for all humanity to get back on track, reconcile with our Father, align with God's plan and loving purposes, and enter into his glorious destiny for us (Rom. 5:12-21). As the second Adam, or representative man, we see in Jesus...

Who God Is

Jesus is the true and complete image and likeness of God. He is "the radiance of God's glory and the exact representation of his being" (Heb. 1:3), so much so that he could make such stupendous claims as "I and the Father are one" (John 10:30—see Appendix A for discussion of this statement) and "anyone who has seen me has seen the Father" (John 14:9). Jesus fully reflected his Father's heart and nature, fully expressed his word and works, and fully revealed his Father's intentions and will. It is in this sense that Jesus is divine or fully godlike (Col. 1:19; 2:9), not in a Trinitarian sense of being "co-equal, co-eternal, consubstantial."

How To Live

Jesus is the ideal, complete, and true man. If you want to know how to live in the Spirit and be "led by the Spirit" (Rom. 8:4-15); if you want to know how to forgive, love your enemies, and overcome evil with good (Rom. 12:21); if you want to know how to be "salt" and "light" and make a positive difference in the world (Matt. 5:13-16); if you want to know how to teach and lead others well (John 13:12-17); if you want to know how much God loves you, and how to live a life of love (John 15:9-13; Eph. 5:1-2); look at Jesus. He is our model, our ideal, our inspiration (Heb. 12:3), so that we can "live as Jesus did" (1 John 2:6).

What We Will Become

Jesus is a declaration and manifestation of our destiny—the goal to which we are moving. He demonstrates the end-state of God's good and loving purposes for us (Ps. 8:3-9; Heb. 2:9-12). "Dear friends, now we are children of God, and what we will be has not yet been made known. But we know that when Christ appears, we shall be like him, for we shall see him as he is" (1 John 3:2).

Jesus is the heavenly man, "not of the world" (John 17:16), whose words are "from above" (John 3:31-36). Likewise, we too are "not of the world" (John 17:16; see also 1 John 2:15) and have already been raised with Christ, positioned alongside him "in the heavenly realms" (Eph. 1:3, 20; 2:6; 3:10). Therefore, we are to set our hearts and minds on "things above, not on earthly things" (Col. 3:2).

Just as Christ is God's son and heir, so we are "heirs of God and co-heirs with Christ," having received the spirit of sonship, by which we cry "Abba, Father" (Rom. 8:15-17). As Jesus was victorious over death, we enter into and share his victory. We too will be glorified, as he now is, in our resurrection bodies (1 Cor. 15:12-58). As Jesus will judge the world and then reign supreme in the messianic kingdom, so too we will judge and reign with him and be given authority even over angels (1 Cor. 6:2-3; Rev. 20:4-6). Jesus is the revelation of who we are becoming: the restored, transformed, perfected, and exalted humanity we will ultimately be.

Jesus truly is the trailblazer—"the pioneer and perfecter of faith" (Heb. 12:2), the "firstborn from the dead" (Rev. 1:5), the "firstfruits" of those who have died and will be made alive (1 Cor. 15:20-23). We are not only to follow in his steps in this life, but will follow in his steps into the future, into the glorious destiny God has prepared for us, by his grace and power, through Christ.

The Jesus of the New Testament is not God, nor an eternal, divine "Person," nor a composite "god-man," but neither is he a mere man. Rather, he is the uniquely begotten Son of the Father, appointed and sent as the promised Messiah to be the Savior of the world and coming king over God's eternal kingdom. He has been glorified above all others, the one to whom every knee will bow, the supreme human Lord under the one Almighty God.

4. Some Objections

There will be some who maintain that to see Jesus as anything less than eternal God is untenable for Christians. I will deal briefly with three common objections:

"JESUS HAD TO BE GOD TO DIE FOR OUR SINS."

This is not taught anywhere in the Bible. In fact, the Bible states very clearly that Jesus had to be a man to die for our sins (Rom. 5:15-19; 1 Cor. 15:21). But this unscriptural notion is based on a couple of unsubstantiated reasons:

The first is that some believe if Jesus were not God himself, or at any rate a "Person" of the Trinity who is fully divine, then the Father would be exacting punishment and payment for our sin on an innocent third party—hardly just or fair. But we need to remember that it was Jesus' choice: he freely and willingly participated in God's redemptive plan, including laying down his life on the cross (John 10:15-17). Christ "loved us and gave himself up for us as a fragrant offering and sacrifice to God" (Eph. 5:2). He could have called on "twelve legions of angels" (Matt. 26:53) to rescue him at any point. However, "For the joy set before him he endured the cross, scorning its shame, and sat down at the right hand of the throne of God" (Heb. 12:2). He will be eternally praised and rewarded for his faith, his love for the Father and for us, his submission and sacrifice.

The second also has no scriptural basis; it is rather a sense many have that one man's death is hardly a worthy sacrifice or adequate atonement for the sins of the world. But we must remember that one (representative) man's disobedience was enough to bring judgment and death on all of humanity. Why wouldn't one (representative) man's obedience therefore be enough to reverse it and redeem us? This is exactly Paul's argument as stated in Romans 5 and 1 Corinthians 15:

> But the gift is not like the trespass. For if the many died by the trespass of the one man, how much more did God's grace and the gift that came by the grace of the one man, Jesus Christ, overflow to the many! (Rom. 5:15)

And after all, isn't it God's prerogative to determine what is an adequate price, an efficacious sacrifice for our redemption?

We also need to remember that this is not any man's death we are talking about, but as outlined above, the death of a unique and special man. He had to be sinless, having no sins of his own to pay for, as foreshadowed in only sacrificial animals without blemish being an acceptable offering in the Old Testament (Lev. 22:21; 1 Pet. 1:19). He was also specially begotten, fully surrendered and dearly loved by the Father.

Some feel that if Jesus isn't God, then his death on the cross is somehow a less loving or significant sacrifice. However, the Bible makes it clear that Jesus' death was a costly and sacrificial act by both the Father and his son (John 3:16; 17:23; Col. 3:2; 1 John 4:14-16). Most parents will tell you: if it came to a choice between watching their child suffer in agony or taking that suffering upon themselves, they would choose the latter.

This objection also raises other problems. We have already seen that the Bible says God is immortal and that, therefore, it is impossible for him to die (Rom. 1:23; 1 Tim. 1:17). So if Jesus is "consubstantial" and inextricably one within the Trinity, how can he be forsaken by God on the cross? And in what way did he die?[4] If he can't "completely" die, do we really have complete atonement for our sins?

---

4. Some try to address this paradox by appealing to the dual nature of Jesus, with only his "human" part dying. For a discussion of why such explanations are problematic, see: "Podcast 145 – 'Tis Mystery All: the Immortal dies!," by Dale Tuggy, *Trinities*, June 27, 2016, https://trinities.org/blog/podcast-145-tis-mystery-immortal-dies/.

"If Jesus isn't God, then we lose everything."

This is a remark I heard recently. It's like other statements that extreme Trinitarians make at times, like that unless you believe in the Trinity you can't be a Christian (or can't be saved). They are based on personal opinion and are without scriptural support.

I believe such comments also reflect a loss of perspective. As far as the focus of the Bible is concerned, of primary importance is Jesus' designation as Messiah and all that means and implies, his character and example, his life and teaching, his mission as sent by God to be the Savior of the world, his atoning death, his resurrection, his ascension to God's right hand, his authorized position as Lord of all and head of the church, the sanctifying work of his spirit, who we are in Christ and all he has called us to be and do as Christ's body in the world, his role as mediator and High Priest, his return in glory to judge the world and to reign over God's kingdom... There are so many issues far more significant than esoteric debates and deliberations around Jesus' ontology.

So what do we really stand to gain or lose if we see Jesus as the Son of God, but not God the Son; as being divine but not deity; as being "of God" (Rom. 3:23) and the "image of God" (2 Cor. 4:4) rather than himself God? Well, some of the things that Trinitarians may "lose" are...

The Concept of the Trinity as a Core Belief and Defining Doctrine of Christianity

I've heard people express that the mystery of the Trinity, its very defying of understanding or logic, somehow demonstrates it must be from God and not of human origin. However, they don't apply the same criteria and logic to other non-scriptural beliefs or to non-sensical ideologies that abound.

Many Christians think the doctrine of the Trinity is of Christian origin. However, it is a matter of historical fact that many ancient pagan religions had divine triads or trinities—Samaria, Babylonia, India, Egypt, Greece, to name a few. In some cases the similarities are striking. This is not a concept unique to Christian theology.[5]

If the doctrine of the Trinity is so definitive, core, and essential to Christianity, why do we see a Trinity-free gospel preached throughout the book of Acts—and to great effect? Surely converts and believers from Pentecost until the Council of Constantinople in AD 381 were truly Christians—with all the faith and beliefs essential to be such— even though we know they did not believe in a tripersonal God.

Using the Trinity as a Model of Christian Community

The Trinity is used as the ultimate example of unity in diversity, mutual interdependence, love, and so forth. However, if Paul or other New Testament writers had a Trinitarian concept of God, why didn't they employ it for illustrative purposes? Instead, they use different models such as the body (1 Cor. 12), marriage (Eph. 5:21-28), family (1 Tim. 5:1-2), and a building (1 Pet. 4:2-60) to explain and illustrate these relational dynamics.

"Trinitarian" Incarnation

The Bible certainly teaches that Jesus fully expresses God the Father. *Yahweh* was in Christ (John 17:20; 2 Cor. 5:19) and the Father was clearly revealed and seen in the Son (e.g., John 8:19; 10:38; 12:45-49; 14:7-11). God's Spirit and word were fully operational in him and manifest through him (John 1:14). But this is very different from the concept of an eternal second person of the Trinity becoming man.

Paul does not hesitate to say that Jesus is the "image of the invisible God" (Col. 1:15), that "God was pleased to have all his fullness dwell in him" (v. 19), and that "in Christ all the fullness of the Deity lives in bodily form" (2:9), because as we've seen, the God Paul refers to is always the Father. Jesus fully reflected his Father. He

---

5. To learn more about these earlier iterations, see "How Ancient Trinitarian Gods Influenced Adoption of the Trinity," Beyond Today, United Church of God, July 22, 2011, https://www.ucg.org/bible-study-tools/booklets/is-god-a-trinity/how-ancient-trinitarian-gods-influenced-adoption-of-the-trinity.

was God the Father fully revealed in a man. In the same way, but to a lesser degree, we, too, are "incarnations" of God and of Christ (see John 17:26; 2 Cor. 3:18; Eph. 2:22; 3:19).

However, when Trinitarians refer to Christ as "God incarnate" they usually conceive of Jesus being a human manifestation of his own personal preexistent "God" self—the second person of the Trinity born and living in human form. Rather than God the Father, or his word and spirit enfleshed in Jesus (John 1:14), they think in terms of "God the Son" enfleshed as a man or becoming a man, beginning as a baby in a manger in Bethlehem.

According to the orthodox Christmas narrative, here is the infinite God "contracted to a span," helpless and vulnerable. Much has been made of this picture, and I admit that it is quite touching and emotionally engaging. But I believe that like other endearing parts of the Christmas script that are not scripturally based, it needs to be consigned to folklore—things like three kings with the shepherds in a stable, the little drummer boy, Santa Claus, and so forth.

The Thought of God Himself Dying For Us

We've already looked at this in our first objection, so I won't reiterate it here.

I accept that Trinitarians have considerable intellectual and emotional investment in their paradigm. To perceive things differently may cause loss and grief. On the other hand, I believe that it would also bring some definite benefits:

A More Clear, Consistent, Coherent, and Compelling Understanding of the Scriptures

When I considered the Non-trinitarian perspective, I found that I no longer had to struggle with anomalies and inconsistencies in logic; no longer had to perform exegetical backflips; no longer had to ignore or explain away certain verses that didn't fit the paradigm. The Bible just started making a whole lot more sense.

A More Real and Relatable Jesus

No longer is he the Jesus of philosophical speculation, the complex Jesus with a composite human-divine nature, an ethereal Jesus who lived on a different plane from us mere mortals. Rather, he is the Jesus who truly experienced our human condition, with all its limitations, struggles, and frailties.[6]

He's the one who can authentically empathize with us, as he was "tempted in every way, just as we are—yet he did not sin" (Heb. 4:15). We are of the same family. "So Jesus is not ashamed to call [us] brothers and sisters" (Heb. 2:11).

In Trinitarian theology, however, there seems to be a hesitancy to focus on the relationship we have with Jesus as our brother. Is that because it makes him seem a little too familiar or human?

A High View of Humanity

I suspect that the focus on the sinful and failed first Adam, to the exclusion of the second sinless and victorious Adam, has skewed our perspective. If Jesus has to be deified to be of any ultimate earthly worth, it devalues our human nature *even further*.

The Bible, on the other hand, declares an exalted position we human beings have in God's creation (Gen. 1:26-28; Ps. 8:3-8), in his calling (John 17:18; 20:21), in his heart (John 15:9; 1 John 3:1), and in his destiny for us (Rom. 8:18-23; 1 Cor. 2:9).

A Refocus on The Father

"Yet a time is coming and has now come when the true worshipers will worship the Father in the Spirit and in truth, for they are the kind of worshipers the Father seeks" (John 4:23).

If you survey the New Testament, you will discover that the prayers, the expressions of praise and thanksgiving, and the hymns and doxologies are overwhelmingly directed to God the Father. This

---

6. To learn more about the historical speculations of Jesus' "two natures," see Dale Tuggy, "Clarifying Catholic Christologies," lecture recording by 21st Century Reformation, July 31, 2017, https://youtu.be/s6wK-lRZP-k.

is in contrast to the evangelical church today, where the majority of praise and thanksgiving (and even prayers and worship songs) are directed to Jesus.

I am not saying that Jesus should not be thanked and praised. But it is a matter of priority and perspective (and theology). I'm not sure how Jesus would feel about his Heavenly Father being so marginalized in worship, when he himself only ever lived to bring focus and glory to "the only true God" (John 17:3). In his book, *The Forgotten Father*, Tom Smail highlights a similar loss of appropriate focus within the charismatic movement to which he belongs, where the Holy Spirit often takes center stage.[7]

Less Complicated Evangelism

Reaching people without faith, or of other faiths, is always a challenging task. The last thing we need is to erect unnecessary barriers that hinder credibility and faith in Jesus and the gospel. Yet that is what the Trinity presents to many.

The Trinity is a blockage for Jews and Muslims who are strictly monotheistic—they see the Christian faith as tri-theism in denial. There is also a steady drip of converts to Islam from Christianity because of this doctrine. Many who convert express relief that they now have a sensible monotheism, whereas before they found the Trinity convoluted and confusing. It is also true of rationalistic or scientifically-minded atheists, who see the concept of three separate persons in one being as contradictory and illogical. And saying to them that it is a mystery which defies human understanding is not very helpful.

An Undiminished Faith

I can appreciate that many Christians cannot contemplate the thought that Jesus is anything other than fully God. It's how they were brought up in the Christian faith. It's how they have always seen

---

7. Thomas A. Smail, *The Forgotten Father* (Grand Rapids, MI: Eerdmans, 1981).

him; what they've always believed him to be. It's how they've always related to him. It may seem like anything other than that perception is unacceptable and would amount to a denial of their faith in Christ or a reduction of his status.

That's where I stood for many years. But ultimately what was more important to me than my Christian heritage, what I thought, or how I felt, was what the Bible says. What do the Scriptures teach? What has Jesus declared, and what has God revealed?

I can honestly say now that my fears were unfounded. I respect, esteem, love, and adore Jesus as much now as ever, and in some ways appreciate him even more than I did before. It hasn't diminished him in my eyes, but only raised my sense of wonder and praise. I see him as totally worthy of my heart's affection, my life's devotion, of highest praise and honor, and of any and every sacrifice I could ever make for him.

I want to close out this chapter with a quotation which some of you will have heard. It will also serve to introduce what I want to present in the next and final chapter. It's from a speech called *That's My King! Do You Know Him?*[8] by S.M. Lockridge, then Pastor of Calvary Baptist Church in San Diego, California. It is a wonderful declaration of praise to Jesus Christ. As you read it (best done in a Southern American accent), realize that everything that is said here can be *equally affirmed* by both Trinitarians and Non-trinitarians alike:

> The Bible says he's the King of the Jews,
> He's the King of Israel,
> He's the King of Righteousness.
> He's the King of the Ages,
> He's the King of Heaven,
> He's the King of Glory,
> He's the King of Kings, and he is the Lord of Lords.
> Now that's my King! Do you know him?

---

8. S. M. Lockridge, "That's My King - sermon by S.M. Lockridge," June 25, 2015, video, https://youtu.be/9K80pozOfrU.

No means of measure can define his limitless love.
Well, well he's enduringly strong,
He's entirely sincere,
He's eternally steadfast,
He's immortally graceful,
He's imperially powerful,
He's impartially merciful.
Do you know him?

He's God's Son,
He's a sinner's Savior,
He's the centerpiece of civilization,
He's unparalleled,
He's unprecedented,
He is the loftiest idea in literature,
He's the highest personality in philosophy,
He's the fundamental doctrine of true theology.
Do you know him?

He supplies strength for the weak,
He's available for the tempted and the tried,
He sympathizes and he saves,
He heals the sick,
He cleansed the lepers,
He forgives sinners,
He discharges debtors,
He delivers the captives,
He defends the feeble,
He blesses the young,
He serves the unfortunate,
He regards the aged,
He rewards the diligent,
And he beautifies the meek,
Do you know him?

My king is the key of knowledge,
He's the wellspring of wisdom,
He's the doorway of deliverance,
He's the pathway of peace,
He's the roadway of righteousness,
He's the highway of holiness,
He's the gateway of glory,
Do you know him?

His life is matchless,
His goodness is limitless,
His mercy is everlasting,
His love never changes,
His word is enough,
His grace is sufficient,
His reign is righteous,
His yoke is easy, and his burden is light.
Well, I wish I could describe him to you, but
He's indescribable,
He's incomprehensible,
He's invincible,
He's irresistible,
You can't get him out of your mind,
You can't get him off of your hand,
You can't outlive him, and you can't live without him.

Well, the Pharisees couldn't stand him, but they found out
they couldn't stop him.
Pilate couldn't find any fault in him.
Herod couldn't kill him,
Death couldn't handle him,
And the grave couldn't hold him.

That's my king—he always has been and he always will be.
I'm talking about he had no predecessor and he'll have no
successor.

You can't impeach him and he's not going to resign.

That's my king!

Summary:

The Bible declares why Jesus is unique in so many ways—the perfect reflection he is of God, the special place he holds in God's heart and purposes for the world, the ideal example he is of how we are meant to live and what we are destined to be.

By God's Spirit, Jesus was divinely chosen, conceived, and commissioned; divinely anointed and appointed, authorized and authenticated, empowered and endowed, infused and inspired. He was totally surrendered and submissive to the Father so that he could fully represent and reflect God's heart, character, and purposes, his will, and his word.

Therefore, God has glorified him above all, giving him a name above every name (Phil. 2:9-11), conferring on him a kingdom (Luke 22:29) and everlasting glory forever and ever (Rev. 5:11-14). Through faith in Jesus Christ, his God and Father can be our God and Father, too (John 20:17, 31), and in him we are positioned and destined to enter into his inheritance, his future and fullness (Rom. 8:16-17).

The Bible teaches that this Jesus came in flesh as a human being. He was born and lived as a man: completely human. He is not a Gnostic or Trinitarian Jesus with a composite nature, a humanity compromised or compartmentalized by his deity.

Such a Jesus would not be genuinely and authentically human. Hence, he could not be truly mortal, tempted and tested, perfected, capable of completely identifying and sympathizing with us. He would be less fully the model, mediator, pioneer, perfecter, brother, and High Priest that the Bible declares him to be.

CHAPTER 7

WHAT'S ESSENTIAL?

EVEN IF YOU ARE NOT convinced with what I have said so far, I encourage you to continue reading. As I said at the beginning, my key intention is not to win the argument, or even necessarily to convince you to see things my way. Rather my key aims are to...

RAISE AWARENESS. Many have only ever been fed the party line, not realizing there's another side to the argument—as well as contrary evidence—when seeking to discern the biblical witness as to who Jesus is and the nature or composition of God. For many years I was certainly in that position.

CHANGE PERCEPTIONS. Those who don't accept Trinitarian theology aren't heretics who ignore the Scriptures and have denied the faith. In fact, all the Non-trinitarians I have come across take the Scriptures very seriously and "contend for the faith that was once for all entrusted to God's holy people" (Jude 3). They are fully committed disciples of Jesus Christ. But rather than being content to simply accept what others say, they have usually arrived at their position after much prayerful, careful research and thorough Bible study. To hold their unorthodox belief has often cost them dearly. They hold their position by conviction, not just convention.

BUILD BRIDGES. Ultimately, I want to appeal for tolerance and grace, mutual respect and love, and for the Christian unity that Jesus prayed for (John 17:20-25) and Paul pleaded for (Eph. 4:1-5) between Trinitarians and Non-trinitarians. I believe this is thoroughly scriptural and reasonable, based on the following:

1. What the Bible states is essential

"Everyone who believes that Jesus is the Christ is born of God, and everyone who loves the father loves his child as well." (1 John 5:1)

Notice that for John, believing that Jesus is the Messiah is the essential criterion for being "children of God" or "born again" (John 1:12; 3:5-8). In John's introduction to his Gospel, he shows that to believe Jesus is the Christ, or the Messiah, is the same as believing "in his name" (John 1:12), in him as "God's Chosen One" (John 1:34), the "Lamb of God" (John 1:36), the "Son of God...the king of Israel" (John 1:49).

John's Gospel and epistles are completely consistent: it is by believing in Jesus that we will not perish but have life in his name (John 3:15-16; 20:31). There is no requirement to also believe that Jesus is himself God or part of the Godhead. As we've seen, there is no clear evidence that John or any of the New Testament writers *ever believed this themselves.*

And even if they did, they never expressed it as an essential of belief or faith in Jesus in order for us to belong to him, to be born again, or to receive eternal life. You will search in vain to find any such requirement in the gospel presentations or responses in the earliest history of the church, the book of Acts.

Theological differences and disagreements are part of the ecclesiastical landscape. There are debates over whether God created the universe in six literal days of 24 hours or a much longer period, over the interplay of God's sovereignty and man's free will, over how secure our salvation is, over what happens when we die, the sequence of events around Jesus' second coming, what eternal punishment looks like, whether it's right for homosexuals to marry, and whether to gather for worship on Saturday or Sunday, just to name a few. While there are always zealots who hold entrenched positions in doctrinal debates and condemn those who differ, generally, Christians adopt a much more gracious approach.

Paul advises the Christians in Rome against "quarrelling over disputable matters" (Rom. 14:1). On controversial issues such as those listed above, we typically form our own personal convictions, including what we believe are good, biblical reasons that support them, and allow others the same freedom to do likewise. We may have different perspectives and arrive at different conclusions, but we respect another's right to his or her opinion. We agree to disagree agreeably.

If those who hold another position acknowledge Jesus Christ as their Lord and Savior, we accept them as fellow believers, albeit with views on some matters that differ from ours. We don't label them as heretics, or believe they have denied the faith. We don't condemn them. We don't demand they change, or else face the risk of being excommunicated, ostracized, or damned.

However, when it comes to disagreement and debate over the theological issue of the Trinity, it's a different ballgame. The above conventions no longer seem to apply. Many put this issue in a different category, seeing it as a core issue, an "essential," a non-negotiable tenet of belief. It's something they will go to the wall for—guns blazing, no ground given, no prisoners taken.[1]

I'm sure in most cases the motivations are genuine and honorable. But over the years, many sincere and devoted Christians have been harshly criticized, ostracized, anathematized, persecuted, even hanged or burned at the stake because their interpretation differed, not from the Bible, but from the orthodoxy of the day.

My appeal is this: let's be careful we don't go beyond what the Bible teaches as essential and condemn our brothers and sisters just because they don't agree with our position on matters that the Bible never presents as crucial.

2.   What we hold in common

If Trinitarians wish to draw upon their concept of the Godhead

---

1. To explore further how essentially (or otherwise) evangelicals hold to the Trinity through their actions, see: "Podcast 286 – Is the Trinity Essential? – Three Views," by Dale Tuggy, featuring a video clip from Dr. William Lane Craig, with a video clip by Dr. James White, *Trinities,* February 17, 2020, https://trinities.org/blog/podcast-286-is-the-trinity-essential-three-views/.

as a model for Christian community, let it serve to highlight the value of complex unity over conformity, of humility and respectful consideration over coercion.

Our natural human tendency is to identify and associate with others based on differences and distinctions. We use the things we share in common, or the things we disagree on, as the criteria upon which we approve or disapprove of others, accept or reject, include or exclude. There is a strong "us-versus-them" mindset behind most of the political, socioeconomic, and even ecclesiastical conflicts around the globe today. We so easily focus on the things that divide, rather than the things that unite.

The unity of all believers, of all devoted disciples of Christ, weighed heavily on his heart as Jesus, facing the cross, interceded for us:

> I pray also for those who will believe in me through their message, that all of them may be one, Father, just as you are in me and I am in you. May they also be in us so that the world may believe that you have sent me. (John 17:20-21)

It weighed heavily on the apostles' hearts as they faced dissension in the early church (Acts 6:1-6). And it certainly weighed heavily on Paul's heart as he addressed the divisions in the Corinthian church (1 Cor. 1:10-17). He exhorted believers to "make every effort to keep the unity of the Spirit through the bond of peace" (Eph. 4:3), by calling on them to focus on the essential things we share in common (Eph. 4:2-6) and our common life in Christ: "There is neither Jew nor Gentile, neither slave nor free, nor is there male and female, for you are all one in Christ Jesus" (Gal. 3:28).

It also weighed heavily on the founders of Churches of Christ, the Stone-Campbell movement to which I belong. They saw the divisions and factional splintering happening in the protestant denominations of their day, often over quite minor points of difference in doctrine or church policy and practice.

Unity was high on their agenda as they declared, "We are

Christians only, not the only Christians,"[2] and called on believers to focus on the things that unite while allowing freedom and mutual acceptance where there were individual differences of opinion and interpretation. Their vision and basis for unity was summed up in this dictum: "In essentials unity, in non-essentials liberty, in all things charity (love)."[3] Another of their mottos expressing a core principle of unity was: "No creed but Christ; no book but the Bible."[4] They saw the divisive nature of creeds and church traditions and sought truth and unity based on the authority of the Scriptures alone.

Carl Ketcherside, a leader in the Stone-Campbell movement, once wrote: "Wherever God has a child, I have a brother or sister." When asked about accepting brothers who were in error, Ketcherside would reply, "That is the only kind of brother that I have."[5]

We noted that the declaration by S.M. Lockridge of the incomparable Jesus as King of Kings is something that both Trinitarians and Non-trinitarians can equally affirm. While we may not see eye-to-eye on everything, we can agree on those things about Jesus that are ultimately significant. And as Rick Warren says: we don't have to see eye-to-eye in order to walk hand-in-hand. I don't want to ignore the theological differences between Trinitarians and Non-trinitarians, or to pretend that they don't matter. But I do want us to keep them in proper perspective.

The other thing that happens when we adopt an adversarial approach, an us-versus-them mentality, is that we stop truly hearing each other or meaningfully engaging in conversation. We practice "selective" listening, where we have our agenda foremost and only listen to see if what the other person says aligns with what we already believe, and if it doesn't, how we can counteract what they are saying.

---

2. Douglas A. Foster et al., eds., *The Encyclopedia of the Stone-Campbell Movement* (Grand Rapids, MI: Eerdmans, 2004), 688.

3. ibid.

4. ibid.

5. Graham Carslake, *DNA of the Churches of Christ Movement* (Xlibris, 2014), 74.

It's not about understanding, it's about winning the argument.

The church councils of the fourth century, through their political posturing and philosophical pontification, through convoluted and schismatic debates around semantics and doctrine, gradually developed and eventually arrived at a theological construct called the Trinity.

This construct took Jesus...

- Beyond being divine to deity,
- Beyond *Elohim* to *Yahweh* (or at least a part of *Yahweh*),
- Beyond "Lord" to LORD (as in the LORD God Almighty),
- Beyond being the "Son of God" to "God the Son,"
- Beyond being the image of God, the representation of God, and the instrument of God, to being himself fully God,
- Beyond being the *logos* enfleshed to being his own preexistent self enfleshed.

In that process, I believe they went beyond what the Scriptures say, and so ended up in conflict with what the Scriptures quite clearly teach, especially in aspects such as the humanity of Christ and his subordinate position to the Father.

However, let's keep this in perspective. When all is said and done, both Trinitarians and Non-trinitarians acknowledge Jesus as "the Messiah, the Son of the living God" (Matt. 16:16). Both have placed their faith in him, committed their lives to him, and seek to follow him as their Lord and Savior. Both love him and are devoted to him, praise and honor him, and seek to adhere to his teaching by walking in his steps.

Based on the authority of God's word and its promises, both are therefore saved by grace (Eph. 2:8-10), belong to Christ (Rom. 1:6) and are children of God (1 John 5:1) and brothers and sisters together—with each other and Jesus (Rom. 8:14-18).

3. Keeping differences in perspective

At the end of the day, how important is the debate over Jesus' deity, as opposed to his divinity? Is it perhaps of greater philosophical interest than actual theological significance? After all, wherever you land on this theology, I assume you still hold to...

- The Scriptures as your authority and divinely trustworthy guide.
- Jesus' life, example, and character as your model and goal.
- His teaching and revelation of God's kingdom as his will for us and the world, as truth to believe and live by.
- Jesus' ministry and miracles as an expression of his Father's approval, power, and compassion.
- Christ's passion and death for our salvation: the struggle of Gethsemane, the desertion of the disciples, the unjust accusations and trials, and the agonizing pain of the thorns, beatings, and crucifixion. The nails are just as sharp and the humiliation just as piercing.
- The historicity of the physical resurrection and ascension of Christ.
- Christ's glorification. Whether you see it as by right or as being conferred by the Father, Jesus still sits at God's right hand, having "the name that is above every name" (Phil. 2:9), with "all authority in heaven and on earth" (Matt. 28:18). He is sovereign Lord of Lords and King of Kings (Rev. 17:14; 19:16), to whom every knee shall bow.
- Jesus as head of the church (Eph. 5:23; Col. 1:18) and as our Great High Priest, the one who mediates and intercedes for us before the Father (1 Tim. 2:5; Heb. 4:15-18).
- Jesus as savior, the only "name under heaven given to mankind by which we must be saved" (Acts 4:12), "the way and the truth and the life. No one comes to the Father except through [him]" (John 14:6).
- Salvation by grace through faith in Christ.
- God's abiding power and presence through the Holy Spirit.
- All the New Testament exhortations to holy and committed living, to a life of love, faithfulness, and integrity, to mission and sacrificial service for others....and so much more.

A person's position on this doctrine impacts very little on the power, principles, and practice of Christian living. Our allegiance to Jesus Christ, our love for God and others, our daily commitment and Christian conduct, are determined by factors beyond our understanding of the interrelationship between Father, Son, and Holy Spirit. And I'm so glad we won't have to pass a theological exam to be accepted into God's kingdom. Church history and current controversy notwithstanding, we need to keep this debate within an appropriate and biblical perspective.

4.   The foundation of our faith

> When Jesus came to the region of Caesarea Philippi, he asked his disciples, "Who do people say the Son of Man is?" They replied, "Some say John the Baptist; others say Elijah; and still others, Jeremiah or one of the prophets."
> "But what about you?" he asked. "Who do you say I am?"
> Simon Peter answered, "You are the Messiah, the Son of the living God."
>
> Jesus replied, "Blessed are you, Simon son of Jonah, for this was not revealed to you by flesh and blood, but by my Father in heaven. And I tell you that you are Peter, and on this rock I will build my church, and the gates of Hades will not overcome it." (Matt. 16:13-18)

To truly understand who Jesus is, I believe we need to be informed, not by popular opinions circulating about him, not by our cherished personal beliefs concerning him, but as we see here—by what the Father has revealed and the Scriptures clearly teach. It is my contention that some of the ideas which are held today (within the Christian community generally and by Christians individually) as to who Jesus is have a human origin—"flesh and blood" (v. 17)—in creeds, rather than in what God the Father has revealed. God's revelation, confirmed by Jesus himself, is that he is the Messiah, the Son of God.

Moreover, this understanding of Jesus was the bedrock upon which Jesus said he would build his church. My simple plea is that we be faithful to what Jesus stipulated in this matter and use *what he designated* as the foundation of belief about him as the basis for Christian faith and unity and for church life and practice.

Unfortunately, this is not how things have played out in church history. Some misinterpreted what Jesus said, taking it to mean that the church would be built on Peter. He was seen to be the first in a long succession of Popes who headed up the Church and spoke *ex cathedra*, with authority to make decisions on matters of church doctrine and practice. History records the excesses and abuses of this power, as well as the corruption that entered the church because of it. Eventually Martin Luther and others opposed what was happening, which led to the Protestant Reformation.

The foundation Jesus refers to is not Peter. Were that what Jesus meant, the Greek word would have been *petros* in the masculine gender. The foundation (*petra*) upon which the church is built and stands is Peter's understanding and declaration of Jesus as the long-awaited Messiah, who is the Son of God. The apostles make it very clear that it is Jesus himself who is not only head of the church, but its foundation as well: "For no one can lay any foundation other than the one already laid, which is Jesus Christ" (1 Cor. 3:11).

In the early centuries of Christianity, there was considerable disagreement over the person of Jesus; the issue of his deity was hotly disputed and vehemently debated. When the Roman emperor Constantine made Christianity the "official" religion, the last thing he needed in a dispersed and destabilized empire was a divided church. He brought a representative group of bishops together in what was to become the first of many such councils, at Nicea in AD 325.

As we've seen, Constantine understood and cared little for the theological issues at play, but did bring pressure to bear to resolve the situation, not through unity, but through conformity and compliance. A statement was formulated, and subsequently further developed, which became the basis for determining who was orthodox and who wasn't.

Those unwilling to sign off on the statement were ostracized and condemned by the church. By the end of the fifth century, it was a civil offence to hold a variant view, a crime which carried the death penalty. That's how the "foundation" for the church became a creed, rather than what Jesus himself prescribed: faith in him as "the Christ, the Son of God."

The simple narrative of the Jewish Messiah was lost in a world of Greek philosophical thought and theological speculation. Jesus became no longer the Son of God, but "God the Son," a second equal and consubstantial person of the "Godhead."

Historically, the doctrine of the Trinity prevailed and became orthodox. Today this doctrine remains deeply ingrained and highly enshrined in Christianity. I see this as an unfortunate departure from the simple witness of the Scriptures as to Jesus' true nature and identity as expressed in the statement above: the Messiah, the Son of God.

Hence the title for this book—a plea to put Christ before creeds as the basis of our faith. Not just historically in time, but *in priority and significance*, Christ is supreme over later ecclesiastical pronouncements about him.

The Synoptic Gospels all bear witness to this confession (Matt. 16:18; Mark 8:29; Luke 9:20), and nothing in their accounts teaches beyond this understanding of Jesus. John states that the purpose of his Gospel account is to prove exactly this understanding about who Jesus is: "... these are written that you may believe that Jesus is the Messiah, the Son of God, and that by believing you may have life in his name" (John 20:31). Note that eternal life is based upon nothing additional to believing that Jesus is the Messiah and God's son.

5.   The focus of Christian faith

"Christ" is not Jesus' surname, as many Christians suppose. Nor is Christ just another name for Jesus. It is actually a title in the Greek that equates to the Hebrew *messiah*, which as we've seen, means the "anointed one."

Every time we say "Jesus Christ" we are affirming in faith and declaring that Jesus is the Christ: God's Messiah and anointed king. This is indeed the focus of faith in Jesus in the New Testament.

We have just noted that it is the foundational statement of faith about him in the Synoptic Gospels, as it is in John's.

On the day of Pentecost, Peter's message was to prove to the gathered crowd that "God has made this Jesus, whom you crucified, both Lord and Messiah" (Acts 2:36). As previously noted, this is the consistent gospel call to faith throughout the book of Acts, as it is in Paul's epistles. To accept that Jesus is the Christ, the Messiah, is to also acknowledge that he is the Son of God (Matt. 16:16; John 20:31), the Lord at God's right hand (Acts 2:36; 3:21; 7:56), the only Savior of the world (Acts 3:17-20; 4:12).

The focus of faith in the New Testament is in Jesus as the Christ, the Messiah. There is no call anywhere for anyone to believe that he is God. I like this quote from one of the esteemed leaders of Churches of Christ in Australia:

> I cannot escape the deep conviction that the essence of Christianity is loyalty to Christ. That is it in a nutshell. Jesus confronted different persons and simply said, "Follow me"...the glory of the early disciples was that they knew Jesus, believed him, and loved him. They did not begin by believing things about him, having opinions and theories concerning him; they began by believing in him... Christianity is essentially a response to a person. This is beyond all the opinions, theories and theologies that find their expression among Christians. We may differ in these areas but if we have grasped essential Christianity we do not divide over them.
>
> For the early Christians who experienced the living encounter of a flesh and blood person, the Jesus, who said "Follow me" was grasped as "The Christ, The Son of the living God" (Matt. 16:18). To them he was unique and absolute as Savior and Lord. To Christians in all ages his cardinal command remains, "Follow me"—and essentially, Christianity is

summed up in loyalty to Him.[6]

6.   What's central and what's not

The Trinity is an inferred doctrine. Nowhere is the word mentioned or the concept explicitly taught in the Bible. If this doctrine is central and vital for Christian belief and practice, why is it not more clearly and prominently presented in the Scriptures? If, as Trinitarians believe, "Jesus is God" is not only true, but a foundational and crucial tenet of Christian faith, why does Jesus never state it? Why do the apostles in the book of Acts never declare it? Why do the New Testament writers never clearly teach it?

As Millard Erickson, himself a Trinitarian, admits:

> [The Trinity] is not clearly or explicitly taught anywhere in Scripture, yet it is widely regarded as a central doctrine, indispensable to the Christian faith. In this regard, it goes contrary to what is virtually an axiom [that is, a given, a self-evident truth] of biblical doctrine, namely that there is a direct correlation between the scriptural clarity of a doctrine and its cruciality to the faith and life of the church.... The question, however, is this. It is claimed that the doctrine of the Trinity is a very important, crucial, and even basic doctrine. If that is indeed the case, should it not be somewhere more clearly, directly, and explicitly stated in the Bible?[7]

Erickson goes on to observe that the doctrine of the Trinity that he subscribes to is only "implied in Biblical revelation...It is unlikely that any text of Scripture can be shown to teach the doctrine of the Trinity in a clear, direct and unmistakable fashion."[8]

6. E. Lyall Williams, *Living Responsibly* (Glen Iris, Victoria: Vital Publications, 1976), 76-77.

7. Millard J. Erickson, *God in Three Persons: A Contemporary Interpretation of the Trinity* (Grand Rapids, MI: Baker Books, 1995), 11, 108.

8. ibid., 109.

How can an implied doctrine with unclear biblical support[9] be considered to be so central, crucial, and indispensable to Christian faith and belief?

7.   The damage caused by division

It's not a nice feeling when people see you as a heretic or as unsaved, when they reject you or simply treat you differently. My local Minister's Fraternal, which I founded and facilitated, excommunicated me when they learned of my Non-trinitarian belief. One minister said I no longer belonged to the faith, and that he would "pray for my soul." When they discovered my variant view, a Christian couple whose marriage I was to officiate decided to find somebody else, as they considered I believed in a "different God" from them. It has caused problems and tensions in relational networks—not just for me, but even for members of my family by association.

More recently, I chose to stand down from my position as Senior Pastor from the local church I planted and grew during the previous 19 years. This was because of possible negative repercussions resulting from my unorthodox beliefs. At the time, I relinquished my vision, my ministry, my means of income, and lost both my Christian community (as I was no longer allowed to attend) and my opportunity to serve elsewhere in my denomination. Even worse, the church itself unravelled and spiralled into controversy, dissension, and division.

Others I know have been similarly judged, rejected, and excommunicated from Christian fellowship. I have family members who have been sent away from their local church. I know of other families where disagreements over this issue have caused tension, conflict, and alienation—some have even been disowned and disinherited.

A friend of mine, a great guy, was engaged to be married to a beautiful young woman. My wife and I had dinner with them the

---

9. To further explore some of the challenges of deducing Trinitarian doctrine from Scripture, see "Podcast 260 – How to Argue that the Bible is Trinitarian," by Dale Tuggy, *Trinities*, May 6, 2019, https://trinities.org/blog/podcast-260-how-to-argue-that-the-bible-is-trinitarian/.

night before she flew to Adelaide to finalize arrangements for their upcoming wedding. Although they differed on this doctrine, there was no questioning their faith, their mutual devotion to God, and their love and delight in each other. But her father was a local church pastor, and his influence was enough to dissuade her from proceeding with the marriage.

I find such responses and judgmental attitudes (which, by the way, can arise in both camps) all very sad. They are disappointing and unnecessary. Jesus advised that "Every kingdom divided against itself will be ruined, and every city or household divided against itself will not stand" (Matt. 12:25). Damage caused by disagreement and division over this issue (and other non-essentials of the faith) has been massive over the years.

My personal inconveniences pale in significance compared to the many over the centuries who've been persecuted, punished, and martyred by the ecclesiastic powers that be. One such example is Michael Servetus, who was condemned and burned at the stake by Calvin for his differing views on this doctrine.[10]

Generally, I have observed that committed Trinitarians have been the more strident and aggressive in their responses to those who hold a different view. I'm not sure why this is. It may be they fear they have more to lose. It may be that they believe they hold the "theological high ground"—that orthodoxy should not be questioned and they have the right and power to defend it. It may be an aggression (or defensiveness) born of insecurity. I'm reminded of the boy who found his pastor's preaching notes. In the margin alongside one point was the comment: "Argument weak. Shout here!"

Whatever the reason, it is certainly the Trinitarians who have done most of the persecuting of Non-trinitarians over the centuries. Which is interesting, considering that Jesus warned his followers that they would be the ones who would be persecuted, not the ones doing the persecuting (Matt. 5:10-12; 24:9; John 15:20; 1 Thess. 3:4; 2 Tim.

---

10. Roland H. Bainton, *Hunted Heretic: The Life and Death of Michael Servetus 1511-1553*, rev. ed. (Providence: Blackstone Editions, 2005).

3:12). The religious leaders of Jesus' day vehemently protected their position of power and tradition against Jesus, and what was seen as a threat to, and departure from, orthodoxy. We need to be careful not to have zeal based on ignorance rather than knowledge (Rom. 10:2), or to think that in mistreating others we are "offering a service to God" (John 16:2).

8. Knowing Jesus

> "Now this is eternal life: that they know you, the only true
> God, and Jesus Christ, whom you have sent." (John 17:3)

Question: what does it mean to "know" God and Jesus? In a Greek philosophical sense, to "know" is about comprehending concepts and being cognizant of information. It's primarily an intellectual exercise of being aware of pertinent facts and understanding particular truths. But the Hebrew mindset was quite different. In it, to "know" is also highly relational and experiential, a term that even described the intercourse and intimacy between husband and wife: "And Adam knew Eve his wife; and she conceived..." (Gen. 4:1 [Authorized (King James) Version]). To the Greek, knowledge was primarily objective and propositional; to the Hebrew it was highly applicable and therefore also subjective and personal.

To know God is to have an appreciation of his personal attributes and qualities—his heart, mind, and will. Then, in deep connection and affection, it is to respond appropriately to him with faith, love and worship, with a submitted heart and committed life:

> Dear friends, let us love one another, for love comes from
> God. Everyone who loves has been born of God and knows
> God. Whoever does not love does not know God, because
> God is love. (1 John 4:7-8)

As John says here, we don't really know God if we are unloving, if we're not living in ways consistent with his heart and character. To know God is not just knowing about God—accepting certain doctrines or concepts pertaining to him. It includes the heart as well as the head; our responses as well as our reason; our behavior as well as our beliefs.

So when seeking to know God, one of the least relevant or important aspects of his nature is its ontological and existential essence. The most important aspects are the relational ones—personal qualities that have to do with how he thinks, feels, and acts—issues of the heart, character, attitudes, disposition, and so forth.

It is in these respects that Jesus fully reflects and represents his Father (2 Cor. 4:4; Col. 1:15; 2:9; Heb. 1:3), such that to see him is to see the Father (John 14:9), to know him is to know the Father (John 14:7), to honor him, believe in him, and receive him is to honor, believe in, and receive the Father (John 3:34-36; 5:23-24). It is in this sense also that believers in Christ share and "participate in the divine nature" (2 Pet. 1:4).

To me, the irony is that while the church councils of the fourth century were arguing semantics over *ousia* and *hypostasis*, while they were contemplating the philosophical conundrums of their differing theologies of the Godhead, they were exhibiting anything but the nature of Jesus and the Father. There was infighting, power politics, anathemas and persecutions, riots and assassinations. While God's nature was being debated, his heart was being ignored and his Spirit grieved.

Let's not judge them too harshly. I wish I could say things are different now, but unfortunately that's not necessarily the case. I often find that around the entrenched positions held by different people concerning the Trinity, there is a lot of pride, defensiveness, ignorance, and fear, with little grace or love. I believe these sound words of advice from the apostle Paul need to be heeded whenever we are discussing controversial doctrines such as the Trinity:

> "We all possess knowledge." But knowledge puffs up while
> love builds up. Those who think they know something do
> not yet know as they ought to know. But whoever loves God
> is known by God. (1 Cor. 8:1-3)

To this church at Corinth racked by dissension and division, Paul later goes on to say, "If I have the gift of prophecy and can fathom all mysteries and all knowledge, and if I have a faith that can move mountains, but do not have love, I am nothing" (1 Cor. 13:2).

We read that Jesus was full of "grace and truth" (John 1:17). Both are important, but sometimes in our focus on the truth, grace is overlooked, so that we are no longer "speaking the truth in love" (Eph. 4:15).

While we may have different understandings about the nature of Jesus in an ontological sense, we can all agree on his nature of love, which expresses the core quality of his character and heart (1 Cor. 13:4-8). Above everything else, Jesus emphasized that loving God and each other is the most important thing: "the first and greatest commandment," upon which "all the Law and Prophets hang" (Matt. 22:38-39). And in the end, isn't that what counts? So our conversations around this subject can be both honest and humble; and while robust, always respectful.

Summary:

I hope you will hear my heart in what I've presented in this book.

MY PLEA is to rediscover the Jesus of the Bible—to remove the overlays of subsequent Greek philosophical thinking and ecclesiological traditions that deified and mystified him—to return to a more genuine and Jewish Jesus, a more historic, holistic, and human Jesus, a less creedal and more credible Jesus, as truly portrayed in the Scriptures.

MY PRAYER is that any differences, dialogue, and debate over this plea be done in the spirit of Jesus. May we truly demonstrate his nature as we discuss his nature. May we reflect his heart, so that in all things we maintain genuine love, mutual respect, and Christian unity.

CONTESTED PASSAGES

THERE ARE SOME KEY passages that Trinitarians rely on heavily to support their doctrine. The translation and interpretation of these passages are contested and the discussion a little complex at times. Hence, they are considered here rather than in the general text.

Old Testament

Isaiah 9:6

For to us a child is born, to us a son is given,
and the government will be on his shoulders.
And he will be called Wonderful Counsellor,
Mighty God, Everlasting Father, Prince of Peace.

This verse is often seen as a messianic prophecy, even though it is not referred to in the New Testament. Two terms are often mistranslated and / or misunderstood:

"Mighty God": This Hebrew term (*el gibbor*) is defined by leading Hebrew lexicons as "divine hero, reflecting the divine majesty," or as "warrior, tyrant, champion, giant, valiant man, mighty man." In the LXX it is translated "messenger of mighty counsel." Other usage reflects these meanings (e.g., Ezek. 17:13; 31:11; 32:21). It is not usually a term or title for God.

"Everlasting Father": Hebrew lexicons give the meaning of everlasting or eternal here as "ongoing, in terms of future duration" (e.g., Ps. 37:29). "Father" in Hebrew parlance is a term of respect, afforded to the patriarchs (Rom. 4:1, 12, 16) and to other esteemed individuals (e.g., 2 Kings 2:12; 5:13; 6:21). A few chapters later, in Isaiah, God's servant Eliakim is called "a father to those who live in

Jerusalem and to the people of Judah" (Isa. 22:21). Hence, in the LXX this messianic phrase is translated as progenitor or "father of the age to come."

In any case, even Trinitarians don't see Jesus as God the Father. This is certainly not a reference to messianic deity.

New Testament

JOHN'S GOSPEL PROLOGUE

In the development of Christology within church history, this is the most crucial, influential, and debated passage of Scripture, bar none. Trinitarians rely on it heavily for their theological construct, and so we will examine it more extensively.

Once again, good hermeneutics and honest exegesis demand that we don't approach this passage with our predetermined ideas as to what we think it means. Rather, our foremost consideration should be: "What was the author seeking to communicate? What would his intended audience have understood from what they read?" The cultural and literary context are key.

Most biblical scholars accept that John's prologue is poetic in genre and therefore rich in metaphor and figurative speech. Also, there is growing agreement among scholars that the prologue borrows heavily from Jewish wisdom literature of the Old Testament and Intertestamental period which was popular at the time. This helps inform the context.

> In the beginning was the Word, and the Word was with
> God, and the Word was God. (v. 1)

There is no reason to capitalize "Word" (Greek: *logos*) other than interpretive bias. The Hebrew counterpart of the Greek *logos* is *dabar*, which often refers to the utterance, instruction, or word of God. In its 1,455 occurrences in the Old Testament, it *never* refers to a person (or angel or conscious spirit). This *logos* encapsulates the plan, purpose, and intention of God from the very beginning.

Elsewhere, when John is expressing proximity of persons,

he uses the Greek preposition *para* (John 1:39; 4:40; 8:38; 14:17, 23, 25; 19:25) and, less frequently, *meta*. So when it says "the word was with God" it is possible, but unlikely, that the Greek phrase *pros ton theon* would have been used in the sense of "alongside."[1] The usual sense of *pros* (+accusative), as here, means "to," "towards," "in reference to," "pertaining to," or " characteristic of." This is how it is translated elsewhere (e.g., Rom. 5:1; 2 Cor. 5:8; Heb. 2:17; 5:1).

However, John does place this *logos* in reference to God, yet in some sense distinguished from him. When this same literary relationship between God and *dabar* occurs in the Old Testament (e.g., Pss. 107:20; 147:15, 18; Isa. 9:8; 55:11), it is to be noted that...

- It always appears in poetic literature.
- It is seen as a personification of God's spoken command.
- This personification is portrayed as an active and independent agent from God, sent on a mission to fulfill his purposes in the world.
- It is often involved in bringing about acts of creation and redemption.

Many of God's attributes are seen to be "with" him (Hebrew: *eim*), and are likewise personified (Job 10:13; 23:14; 27:11; Prov. 2:1-2; Dan. 2:2). Because of the intimate connection between God's word, wise counsel, and instructive understanding, "word" and "wisdom" overlap, and at times are seen as almost synonymous (Job 12:13; Prov. 8:23-30). In Proverbs chapter 8, wisdom is fully personified as a woman, with a personality of her own. She was there "at the very beginning, when the world came to be" (v. 23). She was present when God created the world, "constantly at his side," involved and active in creation and the formation of God's plans for humanity (vv. 27-31).

This same personification of Wisdom is seen in Intertestamental Jewish wisdom literature, such as Sirach (e.g., 1:1), written about 180 BC, and the Wisdom of Solomon (e.g., 9:9) written about 40 BC.

---

1. Sometimes certain qualities are said to be "with" God, but the language is figurative, a personification. See Proverbs 8 in Henry Barclay Swete, ed., *The Old Testament In Greek According to the Septuagint* (Cambridge, MA: Cambridge University Press, 1930).

These books were included in the LXX and were read and well-known by John and early Jewish Christians.

So the personification of God's Word and Wisdom, and their portrayal as being "with God" was very familiar to Jews at the time. However, it needs to be emphasized that even though these attributes were heavily personified, they did not go beyond this to become a person. This Hebraic cultural and literary context should be what informs our Christology, not the determinations of church councils in the fourth and fifth centuries.

When it says, "the word was God," it is significant that the definite article before "God" is omitted. Hence, it can be legitimately translated in three ways:

a. "the word was a god" (as Jehovah Witnesses do)

b. "the word was God" (more common in English versions)

c. "the word was God-like" or "divine"—in an adjectival sense (as in some translations, e.g., translations by James Moffat and William Barclay)

Trinitarian theology has led to the second option being the one often chosen. However, there are some problems with this rendering—linguistically and logically. In terms of Greek grammar, if John had wanted to conflate or collapse the persons here, making the *logos* fully God, he could have expressed it more clearly (e.g., *kai theos ein ho logon*). But even if it is assumed, as Trinitarians do, that "the word" is Jesus, it doesn't make plain sense within the verse—for it would then mean that Jesus is both with God, and is himself the "God" alongside himself (how could that work?). If the first "God" means "Father" (or "Father and Holy Spirit") then the next "God" must carry the same meaning—otherwise it is called "referential inconsistency."

He was with God in the beginning. (v. 2)

Here the Greek word translated "he" is *houtos*, which means "this one" or "that." The Greek word *logos* (word) is masculine in gender, and therefore the pronoun must agree with it. So whether "he" or "it" is selected is a matter of interpretation, as both renderings are possible.

It's interesting to note that the earliest English translations prior to the King James Version all had "it" as the translation: Through *it* (i.e., the word) all things were made; without it nothing was made that has been made. In it was life, and that life was the light of all mankind... (etc., vv. 3-5).[2]

However, even if "he" is selected, this can be understood as a highly personified "word," as we have noted. It does not mean that the *logos* is a deity or a separate person within "God."

> Through him all things were made; without him nothing was made that has been made. (v. 3)

Here we see that God's *logos* is the agent in creation. The Greek verb *ginomai*, which means "to become, happen, come to pass, come to exist," is used three times here, and the same Greek verb is used 23 times in Genesis chapter 1 in the LXX. In fact the opening phrase "*en archē*" (Gen. 1:1 LXX) is repeated here by John. He then goes on to develop parallel themes: the creation of light, life, and the world of human beings. We see similar depictions of God creating through wisdom and his word in the Old Testament:

> By the word of the LORD the heavens were made,
> their starry host by the breath of his mouth. (Ps. 33:6)

> How many are your works, LORD!
> In wisdom you made them all;
> the earth is full of your creatures. (Ps. 104:24)

> By wisdom the LORD laid the earth's foundations,
> by understanding he set the heavens in place;
> by his knowledge the watery depths were divided,
> and the clouds let drop the dew. (Prov. 3:19-20)

---

2. See William Tyndale, *The New Testament* (1526); Myles Coverdale, *Biblia* (1535); Thomas Matthew, *Matthews's Bible* (1537); Myles Coverdale, *Great Bible* (1539); Richard Taverner, *The Epistles and Gospelles with a brief Postyl upon the same* (154); William Whittingham, *The Newe Testament of Our Lord Jesus Christ* (1557); *Geneva Bible* (1560); Lawrence Tomson, *The New Testament of Our Lord Jesus Christ, Translated out of Greeke* (1583).

As Dr. Dustin Smith notes:

> John 1:3 is not making the personified Logos the creator. The wording is very clear. All things came into being through the Logos. The only true God, the Father, is the creator, and God used the Logos as the vehicle through which all things came into being. God is the source, and the personified Logos is the agent.[3]

This aligns and accords completely with Pauline theology in terms of the new creation (e.g., 1 Cor. 8:5-7; Col. 1:16). John is drawing from imagery in Genesis of God's personified utterance, not an archangel or the supposed preexistence of a second member of the Trinity.

> In him was life, and that life was the light of all mankind. The light shines in the darkness, and the darkness has not overcome it. There was a man sent from God whose name was John. He came as a witness to testify concerning that light, so that through him all might believe. He himself was not the light; he came only as a witness to the light. (John 1:4-8)

Here John introduces themes that are developed later in his Gospel, where Jesus continues to function as the light of the world (8:12), speaking the saving words of God that offer life in the age to come.

John the Baptist is a prominent figure in the Gospels, with his long-lasting and widespread influence extending to Ephesus and elsewhere in the Roman Empire even years after his death (e.g., Acts 18:25; 19:1-4). However, his sole role in John's Gospel is to bear witness to God's *logos*, freely confessing he himself is not the Messiah (1:20). His mission? To prepare the way and point to the one beyond himself (1:15).

---

3. See "118: John 1:3 and Creating Through Word and Wisdom," by Dustin Smith, *The Biblical Unitarian Podcast*, April 30, 2020, 6:15 min, https://biblicalunitarianpodcast.podbean.com/e/118-john-13-and-creating-through-word-and-wisdom/.

> The true light that gives light to everyone was coming into
> the world. He was in the world, and though the world was
> made through him, the world did not recognize him. He
> came to that which was his own, but his own did not receive
> him. Yet to all who did receive him, to those who believed
> in his name, he gave the right to become children of God—
> children born not of natural descent, nor of human decision
> or a husband's will, but born of God. (John 1:9-13)

Once again, John draws on Jewish wisdom and Torah tradition, which
spoke of God's wisdom and instruction coming to earth, dwelling
among men, and interacting with God's people (Ecclus. 24:7-12;
Bar. 3:37-4:2; 1 Enoch 42:1-2). This creative and powerful Wisdom
and Word of God continues to function as the *logos*, when in the
world, in and through Jesus. This is expanded further in verse 14.
Biblical scholars have noted the parallelism within John's prologue,
with it's chiastic structure highlighting the central theme to receive
Jesus and believe in his name, expounded throughout the narrative
(2:23; 3:16-18; 17:6) and summarized in his statement of intent
(20:30-31).

> The Word became flesh and made his dwelling among us.
> We have seen his glory, the glory of the one and only Son,
> who came from the Father, full of grace and truth. (John
> 1:14)

Here, "made his dwelling" (Greek: *skēnoō* to dwell, to tabernacle,
to live, to encamp) is the exact word used in Jewish literature for
personified Wisdom dwelling among God's people (Ecclus. 24:7-8). It
introduces John's tabernacle or temple theme, where Jesus functions
as the new temple (John 2:19-22; 4:19-26; 7:14-15; 10:23-25). As with
the temple, Wisdom is associated with God's glory (Prov. 8:18; Wisd.
of Sol. 7:15; 9:11; Ecclus. 4:13; 6:31). This helps us to understand
such statements as, "And now, Father, glorify me in your presence
with the glory I had with you before the world began" (17:5). Jesus,
who is often portrayed in the Gospel narrative as Wisdom's messenger,

continues the purpose of Wisdom as the new temple, revealing and declaring the glory of God (Matt. 11:25-27; Luke 7:31-35; 11:49-51).

To meditate on Proverbs chapter 8 is to appreciate and understand the extent to which Jewish wisdom literature was comfortable with stretching the boundaries of personification as an attribute of God.

Nowhere in this Gospel prologue does John say that the Word is the pre-human Jesus or indicate they are the same self. Nowhere does he subsequently record Jesus saying, "I am the Word," or "God created the world through me."

In conclusion, as a number of biblical scholars[4] believe, John's poetic prologue never intended the "word" to be seen as a personal, deified being. The earth-shattering assertion comes in verse 14, where John marks the "transition from impersonal personification to an actual person. Here God's utterance or manifestation does not merely come through an individual, but is actually manifested in that person, Jesus of Nazareth."[5] It is here that the personified Word becomes the "personed" Word: the man Jesus.

Therefore, the incarnation is not as Trinitarians have conceived it: God becoming enfleshed as a human. Rather, in John 1:14 it is God's *logos*, his Word and Wisdom, that was enfleshed in a human being, Jesus—the one who is uniquely God's Son by virtue of his special birth, calling, and anointing.

The Greek *monogenes* (rendered "only begotten") carries the sense of "unique: the only one in its category." In his prologue, John is not writing about a deified entity called "Word" who existed from eternity and who descended to earth and lived as a man. Not only is such a notion out of alignment with the Old Testament and the Synoptics, but with John's own expressed purpose for his Gospel:

---

4. To explore further, see "Podcast 301 – Dr. Daniel Boyarin on John 1," by Dale Tuggy, *Trinities*, July 20, 2020, https://trinities.org/blog/podcast-301-dr-daniel-boyarin-on-john-1/; "Podcast 298 – Andrews Norton on John 1," by Dale Tuggy, *Trinities*, June 15, 2020, https://trinities.org/blog/podcast-298-andrews-norton-on-john-1/.

5. James D. G. Dunn, *Christology in the Making* (London: SCM Press, 1989), 24.

"But these are written that you may believe that Jesus is the Messiah, the Son of God, and that by believing you may have life in his name" (John 20:31).

John 1:18

> No one has ever seen God, but the one and only Son, who
> is himself God and is in closest relationship with the Father,
> has made him known.

This is a poor translation. "...who is himself God" has been added. It does not appear in the Greek text! However, there is textual uncertainty, reflected in different translations, as to whether the original would have been "only begotten Son" or "only begotten God." "Only begotten Son" seems far more likely:

- It has wider manuscript support.
- When John uses this expression elsewhere (John 1:14; 3:16; 3:18; 1 John 4:9), he is always referring to the Son.

- How would a first-century audience have made sense of an "only begotten God"?
- How would an only unique "God" stand in relation to another "God," the Father?

Preexistence:

There are a number of statements in John's Gospel that, at face value, would seem to support the idea that Jesus personally existed in heaven prior to his birth and came down from heaven to become a man (1:15, 30; 3:13; 6:27-63; 8:58; 17:5, 24). But do John and Jesus mean for these to be understood literally?

A feature of the Johannian Jesus is that he employed metaphors constantly. For example, Jesus spoke to Nicodemus about being "born again," which he used in a spiritual sense (3:3ff). Towards the end of Jesus' ministry, he explained to his disciples, "Though I have been speaking figuratively, a time is coming when I will no longer use this kind of language but will tell you plainly about my Father" (John 16:25).

He goes on to explain his "sending" as (literally in the Greek), "coming forth out of the Father," and going "to the Father." Jesus' disciples responded to this by saying, "Now you are speaking clearly and without figures of speech" (John 16:29). Below are some examples where a figurative understanding is in order:

John 3:2

Rabbi, we know that you are a teacher who has come from God. For no one could perform the signs you are doing if God were not with him.

Being "sent" is a key concept in John, an idea he mentions over 40 times. It doesn't mean being physically or literally sent from heaven; in the Jewish understanding it meant to be authorized and commissioned by God to undertake a mission, as used of John the Baptist (John 1:6). It is to be prophetically sent. Nicodemus, for instance, did not have preexistence in mind when he told Jesus "you have come from God." To "come from" God is the same as being sent by God (John 8:42; cf. Luke 7:16).

John 6:25-65

For the bread of God is the bread that comes down from heaven and gives life to the world. (v. 33)

Many see a reference to Jesus' preexistence in these words, yet the language in Jesus' discourse here is rich in metaphors. As he was "the living bread that came down out of heaven" (v. 51, see also vv. 41, 58), people needed to "eat [his] flesh...and drink his blood" (vv. 53-58) in order to share in eternal life. In verse 63, Jesus explained that he was speaking figuratively.

John 3:13

No one has ever gone into heaven except the one who came from heaven—the Son of Man.

(and)

John 8:23

You are from below; I am from above. You are of this world;
I am not of this world.

In both John 3:13 and 8:23 Jesus is speaking to the religious
establishment. If he meant he literally came from heaven, then to
be consistent he would be saying his opponents literally came from
below, from *Sheol,* or the underworld. These terms don't refer to a
literal origin, but a spiritual reality. His *connection* is with God and
heaven, whereas theirs is with the devil and hell (e.g., John 8:44). Paul
employs similarly metaphorical language when he speaks of Adam as
"the earthly man" and Jesus as "the heavenly man" (1 Cor. 15:49).

John 1:15

John testified concerning him. He cried out, saying, "This is
the one I spoke about when I said, 'He who comes after me
has surpassed me because he was before me.'"

We know that John was six months older than his cousin Jesus, so
how can Jesus be "before" him? Some would say this points to
Jesus' preexistence. Here, the Greek word translated "before" is
ambiguous—it can mean being first or having priority, either in time
or in rank (as in the title of this book!).

If John intended to refer to time, this has been addressed in our
previous discussion on the Hebrew understanding of preexistence
and John's use of the personification of logos in his prologue.[6] But if
the word rendered "before" refers to priority, we should know that in
ancient times, greater respect would normally be afforded the older
person over the younger. Here, John declares Jesus has superiority
over himself (1:27; 3:30).

John 17:5

And now, Father, glorify me in your presence with the glory
I had with you before the world began.

---

6. See chapter 4 for discussion of the Jewish concept of preexistence and the Jewish literary
personification of wisdom.

(and)

John 17:24

Father, I want those you have given me to be with me where I
am, and to see my glory, the glory you have given me because
you loved me before the creation of the world.

These references are to a conceptual, rather than actual, existence. In
a similar way, Paul speaks about that which "God destined for our
glory before time began" (1 Cor. 2:7). This has been covered in our
previous discussion on the Jewish concept of preexistence, but is also
demonstrated in passages such as Ephesians 1:4 and 1 Peter 1:20. In
Jewish understanding, the *Shekinah* glory was predestined for the
Messiah, whom John presents as the new temple (1:14; 2:19-22;
4:19-26; 7:14-15; 10:23-25).

In summary, we can interpret these passages in John literally
within a Trinitarian paradigm, but the result seems dissonant with the
textual and cultural context. On the other hand, we can interpret them
in a metaphorical and proleptic sense, which seems more consistent
with John's bookends of his prologue and his purpose statement.
The latter interpretation has greater congruency with the historical
context and linguistic style as well as the rest of the biblical witness
that was presented in chapter 5.[7]

Jesus' Claims:

Jesus makes many amazing claims about himself in John's Gospel:
He is "the good shepherd" (10:11), "the light of the world" (8:12),
"the way and the truth and the life" (14:6), and so forth. Trinitarians
believe that these claims point beyond him being just the Messiah to
him being equal to God the Father. They see this as especially the case
when Jesus made the following two statements: "before Abraham was
born, I am" (8:58), and "I and the Father are one" (10:30).

---

7. For further discussion around preexistence, see "Podcast 235 – The Case Against
Preexistence," by Dale Tuggy, *Trinities,* July 16, 2018, https://trinities.org/blog/podcast-235-
the-case-against-preexistence/.

John 8:58

Jesus answered, "before Abraham was born, I am!"

Notice that Jesus did not say, "Before Abraham was born, I was," in the sense of a personal preexistence. Nor did Jesus say, "Before Abraham was, 'I AM WHAT I AM'." Some read into this statement *Yahweh*'s name given to Moses (Exod. 3:14), but the Hebrew and Greek texts of that verse (LXX *ego eimi ho on*) are very different. The exact phrase used by Jesus here (*ego eimi*) is also used several other times in John's Gospel:

> I, the one speaking to you—I am **he**. (4:26)

> I told you that you would die in your sins; if you do not believe that I am **he**... (8:24)

> When you have lifted up the Son of Man, then you will know that I am **he**... (8:28)

> But [the blind man] himself insisted, "I am **the man**." (9:9)

The bolded words in these verses, "he" or "the man," are italicized in many translations because these words are *not found* in the Greek text. They are inferred, and therefore added, to make sense of the statement. The same applies here in John 8:58, but on this occasion, interpretive bias has left out "he."

Jesus is simply saying that before Abraham was, I am *he—the Messiah*. In answer to his opponents' previous statement, Jesus was making the point that it was Abraham who saw him, the Messiah, in faith, as he looked forward to the fulfillment of God's promise of blessing through his seed. Paul gives extended commentary on this very point about Abraham's faith in the Messiah (Rom. 4:1-25; Gal. 3:15-29).

John 10:30

I and the Father are one.

This should not be interpreted ontologically but intentionally—understood as "being like-minded, having the same love, being one in spirit and of one mind" (Phil. 2:2; cf. Acts 4:32). It is only in this sense that Jesus' further statements in John make sense: that Christians are to "be one, as we [Father and Son] are one" (John 17:11; see also 17:21-23).

In this passage, the Jewish leaders were seeking a plain statement from Jesus that he was the Messiah (v. 24). He replied that his words and works had testified about him, but because they were not his sheep, they were unwilling to hear or accept it. It is in this context that Jesus made this statement.

The Greek word translated "one" here is neuter (*hen*) and refers to the works or ministry Jesus had just been talking about. Ontology is the study of metaphysics that deals with *the nature of being*, so to assume that this was an ontological statement about he and the Father sharing one essence is to read back into the text what was not intended.[8]

If the personhood of God was being considered, the word for "one" would have been masculine in the Greek (*heis*) as it is elsewhere (e.g., Gal. 3:28; Eph. 4:6). Jesus went on to clarify this statement: he is "God's Son" (v. 36), and "the Father is in me, and I in the Father" (v. 38).

The Jewish leaders considered such an audacious claim— that he was fully aligned and in total harmony with God—to be blasphemous, "because you, a mere man, claim to be..." (v. 33) Here again, as we saw in John 1:1, there is no definite article in the Greek, so we have three options for translation: "God," "a god," or "godly / divine." Even though "God" is the option chosen by the majority of modern translations, it seems unlikely, because:

- It is historically and culturally anachronistic: *no Jew in Jesus' day* would have conceived of the Messiah or any human claiming to be the one supreme *Yahweh*.
- As noted previously, the word "god" had a much more fluid meaning in both Hebrew and Greek literature than it does for us today (e.g., 1 Cor. 8:6; 2 Cor. 4:4).

---

8. For further insight, see "Jesus's argument in John 10," by Dale Tuggy, *Trinities*, November 14, 2014, https://trinities.org/blog/jesuss-argument-in-john-10/.

- Jesus appears to be using the religious leaders' interpretation of Psalm 82:6 against them in his comeback reply (vv. 34-38). By their designation of men as "gods" in that Psalm, he deflects their charge against him.
- Perhaps in the reference here in Psalm 82, and certainly elsewhere (e.g., Exod. 22:8), leaders who were functioning for God are called by that title. This is the principle of agency, which we have previously discussed in chapter 4.
- At his trial, even Jesus' claim to be Messiah was "blasphemy" to the Jewish leaders, a crime punishable by death (John 19:7; Matt. 26:63-66; Mark 14:62-64).

John 20:28

Thomas said to him, "My Lord and my God!"

In our English translation this seems like Thomas is conferring deity on Jesus. But there are reasons to refrain from coming to this conclusion too hastily.

First, with the flexibility of terminology in common usage at the time, it is far from linguistically certain that Thomas is calling Jesus Almighty God here (as noted in chapter 4). Even though John penned these words in Greek when he wrote the Gospel, we need to remember that it is highly unlikely they were spoken in Greek by Thomas. He would have been far more likely to express them in his native tongue (by virtue of typical human nature, and by what is implied in the text itself, where it mentions the use of common native speech. See John 19:13, 17, 20; 20:16).

If Thomas spoke these words in Hebrew, he could have said either "My LORD and my God" (*Adonai* and *Yahweh*), saying Jesus was Almighty God, or he could have said, "My Messiah and Majesty" (*Adoni* and *Elohim*) declaring Jesus to be the (human) Messiah and king of the Jews. If Thomas spoke in Aramaic, both options are still possibilities—*marya*, "Lord God" or *mari*, "my human Lord."

Which of these two options is the more likely? The context is key in answering that question. Just prior to Thomas' statement, we have Jesus' words to Mary after she recognized him in the garden:

> Jesus said, "Do not hold on to me, for I have not yet ascended to the Father. Go instead to my brothers and tell them, 'I am ascending to my Father and your Father, to my God and your God.'" (John 20:17)

Jesus refers to God as his Father and ours, and fully identifies with us in the nature of our relationship to him. Then, immediately after Thomas' interaction with Jesus, John goes on to state his purpose for his Gospel, including his own understanding of Jesus' nature:

> Jesus performed many other signs in the presence of his disciples, which are not recorded in this book. But these are written that you may believe that Jesus is the Messiah, the Son of God, and that by believing you may have life in his name. (John 20:30-31).

Given the immediate context of John's account and the wider context and convention of the designation "God" in the New Testament, it seems highly improbable that Thomas is conferring deity upon Jesus. It is far more likely that Thomas was affirming and declaring Jesus as the "Messiah, the Son of God," the appointed king and victorious Lord in God's kingdom—as now conclusively demonstrated by his resurrection.

The only other place in the New Testament where Jesus is clearly referred to as "God" is in Hebrews 1:8-9, in a quotation from Psalm 45:6-7:

> Your throne, O God, will last for ever and ever; a scepter of justice will be the scepter of your kingdom. You have loved righteousness and hated wickedness; therefore God, your God, has set you above your companions by anointing you with the oil of joy.

Biblical scholars of all persuasions see this psalm as addressed to a human king as God's representative. Here, *Elohim* is applied as a title to Jesus, but note that there is another "God" over him, again underscoring the relative nature of this Hebrew title.

On all other occasions in the New Testament (barring disputed texts), "God" (*ho Theos*) refers *exclusively* to the Father over 1,300 times. As far as the designation of that title in the New Testament is concerned, if Thomas did see Jesus as fully God, it would have been the exception.

Professor Bill Schlegel shows how the interpretation of Thomas' statement here as a declaration of Christ's deity ignores and contradicts Jesus' teaching throughout John's Gospel.[9] Among other things, a "deity of Christ" interpretation...

- Overlooks the response of the other apostles to Jesus' resurrection. To them, this was not proof Jesus was God, but that the Father had raised him to life, confirming Jesus' status as the Messiah (Acts 2:22; 1 Cor. 1:23; 2:2; 15:3-6, 12; 1 Pet. 1:21; etc.).
- Fails to appreciate the degree to which the Father is said to be "seen" in the Son, not in a physical sense (John 1:18), but figuratively: "The one who looks at me is seeing the one who sent me" (John 12:45; see also 10:6; 14:9; 16:25, 29). The consistent biblical teaching is that the one God (the Father) is perceived, seen, and made known in his acts among humankind: "You were shown these things so that you might know that the LORD is God; besides him there is no other" (Deut. 4:35; see also Isa. 43:10).
- Ignores the literary context of Thomas's statement in the Gospel of John:

    i. The previous conversation between Jesus and Thomas, which was all about Jesus revealing the Father (John 14:5-12)

9. Bill Schlegel, "My Lord and My God—Trinitarians Got it Wrong, John 20:28," video presentation, April 25, 2020, https://www.youtube.com/watch?v=hxYp4n52P8Q; also see "John 20:28," The Trinity Delusion, June 11, 2018, http://www.angelfire.com/space/thegospeltruth/TTD/verses/john20_28.html.

ii. The declaration of the resurrected Jesus that his God and Father is the same God and Father of the apostles (John 20:17)

iii. John's statement of purpose (to show that Jesus is the Messiah, not that he is God), which appears only two verses after Thomas's declaration

Trinitarians claim Thomas saw "God the Son" in Jesus. But Jesus said that it was God the Father who was in him (John 8:40; 10:38; 14:9-10; 17:3). This is a serious misidentification, as it ignores and contradicts the consistent teaching of John's Gospel that the Father is the one who is both *at work in Jesus and revealed in Jesus.*[10]

PAUL'S EPISTLES

Romans 9:5

Theirs are the patriarchs, and from them is traced the human ancestry of the Messiah, who is God over all, forever praised! Amen.

This NIV version adds the following as alternative translations in footnotes: "or 'Messiah, who is over all. God be for ever praised!' Or 'Messiah. God who is over all be for ever praised!'"[11] These are equally legitimate, as the Greek text here is ambiguous as to whether the praise is directed to God over Christ or to Christ as God.

As in other instances, for understanding the author's intent the best recourse is to consider the context. We have already examined the wider context of Paul's Christology. Paul consistently calls the Father "God" and Jesus "Lord," and the Father is always seen as superior to the Messiah. Significantly, the other doxologies in this letter (and

---

10. For further discussion on this point, see: Kermit Zarley, "Thomas said to Christ, 'My Lord and My God.' He meant 'God in Christ,' to which We Should Nod," *Kermit Zarley Blog, Patheos,* November 7, 2013, https://www.patheos.com/blogs/kermitzarleyblog/2013/11/thomas-said-to-christ-my-lord-and-my-god-he-meant-gods-in-christ-to-which-we-should-nod/.

11. Taken from *The NIV Study Bible,* ed. Kenneth L. Barker (Grand Rapids, MI: Zondervan, 1995).

generally in Paul's letters) are all addressed to God the Father, not Jesus (1:25; 11:33-36; 16:26-27).

The immediate context is Paul's anguish over his fellow Jews who, in spite of their heritage, have rejected their Messiah. It would seem dissonant, insensitive, and even counter-productive to then give praise to the Messiah as *Yahweh*, which was not part of their heritage. But in any case, this uncertainty means this is not a verse to be used to build a case for the deity of Christ.

Philippians 2:5-11

In your relationships with one another, have the same mindset as Christ Jesus: Who, being in very nature God, did not consider equality with God something to be used to his own advantage; rather, he made himself nothing by taking the very nature of a servant, being made in human likeness. And being found in appearance as a man, he humbled himself by becoming obedient to death—even death on a cross! Therefore God exalted him to the highest place and gave him the name that is above every name, that at the name of Jesus every knee should bow, in heaven and on earth and under the earth, and every tongue acknowledge that Jesus Christ is Lord, to the glory of God the Father.

Biblical scholars generally agree this was part of an early Christian hymn, and hence, like John's prologue, its language is more poetic. Trinitarians often quote these verses because they believe it teaches a personal, preexistent Christ, who humbled himself in the incarnation by becoming a man and dying on the cross. But as always, before we jump to conclusions, assumptions and context need to be checked.

Firstly, the context is not about divine attributes or privileges but about personal attitudes and actions. Outside of this passage, the only other New Testament occurrence of the Greek word *morphe* or its derivatives is when Paul talks about his travail until Christ is formed (*morphothe*) in the Galatian believers (Gal. 4:19). It's about their Christlike character. It's *not* about what Jesus supposedly did in heaven, but how he lived on earth, and how his is an appropriate and relevant example for us to follow.

Biases in interpretation and translation often reveal translators' assumptions. Two Greek terms in this passage have come under intense scrutiny. The first is in verse 6: *en morphe theou*—literally, "in [the] form of God." While some believe this may include the inner nature of something, most reputable sources strongly favor the meaning that refers to its outward appearance or shape.[12]

This latter understanding is overwhelmingly confirmed by its usage in the LXX, Apocrypha, and secular manuscripts of the time. The rendering "in very nature God" as above in the NIV (or similar in some other translations), is not supported: a clear bias. In poetic style, this term "form of God" equates to "likeness" or "image of God" (Deut. 4:16, 23, 25) and hearkens back to mankind's original formation in God's image (Gen. 1:26).

The Greek verb in verse 6, *harpagmon*, does not imply Jesus letting go of what he already had, but along with the Greek sentence construction, expresses "to grasp," or to take hold, of what he did *not* have. In fact, the Greek text goes on to make it quite clear: "for this reason precisely" (*dio kai*) God has exalted Jesus to the highest place of supreme lordship. If, as assumed by Trinitarians, Jesus already had such a position before his birth, this would hardly have been a reward or earned promotion. But here, as elsewhere, it is God who has "conferred" upon Jesus a kingdom (Luke 22:29) and "given" him the name and authority above every other (Matt. 28:18; see also Eph. 1:20-22; Col. 1:18)—ultimately all to "the glory of God the Father" (Phil. 2:11).

The other disputed Greek term is in verse 7: *eauton ekenosen*—

---

12. See Walter Bauer, Frederick Danker, William Arndt, and F. Wilbur Gingrich, *A Greek-English Lexicon of the New Testament and Other Early Christian Literature*, 3rd ed. (Chicago: University of Chicago Press, 2002), henceforth BDAG; Joseph Henry Thayer, *Greek–English Lexicon of the New Testament*, (New York: Harper & Brothers, 1889); Gerhard Kittel, Gerhard Friedrich, and Geoffrey W. Bromiley, *Theological Dictionary of the New Testament: Abridged in One Volume*; *A Greek-English Lexicon of the New Testament and Other Early Christian Literature*; (Grand Rapids, MI: Eerdmans, 1985).

Jesus literally "himself emptied." What was being emptied here? Some assume that it is Jesus emptying himself of some of his divine attributes, or perhaps of his divine rights and privileges, prior to his birth. But even if it is interpreted along these lines, it could apply just as easily to Jesus' messianic privileges on earth (Matt. 20:28; 26:53) as to any supposed divine privileges in heaven.

Significantly, the only other time this phrase appears in the Bible is in the prophecy about Jesus' humiliation and suffering in Isaiah 53:12 "...he poured out his life unto death." I believe this is the best understanding of the term: Jesus "self-emptied" unto death.

Then, as we look at the context, we have already been introduced to Paul's "Second Adam" theology, where he compares and contrasts the two specially formed, representative humans: Adam and Christ (Rom. 5:12-21; 1 Cor. 15:21-22, 45-47). Although contested, a number of biblical scholars see this as another example:

- Jesus, like Adam, was in the form (image, likeness) of God.
- Unlike Adam, Jesus did not seek to "grasp at" or attain equality with God illegitimately.
- Rather than Adam's presumption, pride, and self-advancement, Jesus chose the path of humility, surrender, and submission.
- In contrast to Adam's rebellion, Jesus chose obedience and faithfulness to God—even to the point of a painful and humiliating crucifixion.
- As a result of his pride and rebellion, Adam was cursed and humbled by God. As a result of his humility and submission, Jesus was blessed and glorified by God: "For those who exalt themselves will be humbled, and those who humble themselves will be exalted" (Matt. 23:12; see also Luke 14:11; 18:14).

Colossians 1:15-20
The Son is the image of the invisible God, the firstborn over all creation. For in him all things were created: things in heaven and on earth, visible and invisible, whether thrones

or powers or rulers or authorities; all things have been created through him and for him. He is before all things, and in him all things hold together. And he is the head of the body, the church; he is the beginning and the firstborn from among the dead, so that in everything he might have the supremacy. For God was pleased to have all his fullness dwell in him, and through him to reconcile to himself all things, whether things on earth or things in heaven, by making peace through his blood, shed on the cross.

Trinitarians will often use these verses to "prove" the deity and personal preexistence of Jesus, but as always, we need to leave our assumptions at the door and make sure we are reading Paul's words in context.

In his book, *Surprised by Hope*, N.T. Wright focuses on not just the historical event of the resurrection, but its eschatological implications. He sees the resurrection as the defining event and precursor of a new heaven and new earth, which is already inaugurated and present within the cosmos, brought about by God through the Messiah, and of which Christ has the supreme place of honor. He says that Jesus' resurrection is the start of a new world, a new creation, in which Jesus is already reigning and ruling as Lord.[13]

Notice that prior to this passage, Paul has been speaking in exactly these terms—the spiritual kingdom of God's Son in which we now share through our redemption and forgiveness of sins (vv. 13-14). Note also that the "all things" (*ta panta*) that are created (v. 16) and reconciled (v. 20) are "things in heaven and on earth, visible and invisible, whether thrones or powers or rulers or authorities." These include *invisible* and *spiritual* realities, a clear reference to the new creation and world order, not the material creation of Genesis chapter 1. Peter expresses the same understanding when he speaks of "the resurrection of Jesus Christ, who has gone into heaven and is at God's right hand—with angels, authorities and powers in submission to him" (1 Pet. 3:21-22). This new spiritual order frames our context for understanding.

---

13. N. T. Wright, *Surprised by Hope: Rethinking Heaven, the Resurrection, and the Mission of the Church* (2008; repr., New York: HarperOne, 2018).

In verse 15 Jesus is called literally (*eikon* without the definite article) an "image of the invisible God"—which is very different from him being God. Jesus fully reveals and reflects the Father's heart and character, words and works. He made visible what is invisible, so that he could say that to see him was to see his Father (John 14:9). "The Son is the radiance of God's glory and the exact representation of his being" (Heb. 1:3).

However, just as my image, be it reflected in a mirror or captured in a photo, expresses me and represents what I am like—*but is not me*—so it is with Jesus. An image or representation is not the actual person, nor necessarily part of that person's being.

Jesus is also called the "firstborn over all creation." From its Hebrew heritage, "firstborn" means the eldest son in the family. Elsewhere Paul says we have been "predestined to be conformed to the image of his Son, that he might be the firstborn among many brothers and sisters" (Rom. 8:29). Again, this must be referring to the new creation, because we become God's children and Jesus' brothers and sisters by being "born again" (John 3:3; see also 1:12).

Also, the Greek here (*pases* + genitive) should be translated the "firstborn *of* all creation." The bias in translation attempts to separate Jesus from the rest of the created order—a problem created by not discerning the new creation as the context. However, the common Trinitarian rendering of these verses creates a dilemma where Jesus, the supposed creator of all things, is also the firstborn of his own creation.

This is further reinforced when compared with Jesus being "firstborn from among the dead" (v. 18). As the first man ever to be raised to immortality, Christ is the first man of God's new creation. "Firstborn" can refer to first in time or first in rank and honor. There is some debate about which is meant here, but both apply.

Verse 16 elaborates further by giving the reason, with the connecting word (*hoti*) "for" or "because" or "since"—"in him all things were created." Some versions have "by him" in an effort to give the impression that Jesus is the creator. This is not supported by the Greek (*en auto* + dative), which expresses intention: "because of him," "on account of him," or "with him in view." That's how this phrase is translated consistently everywhere else in the New Testament, including verse 19 in this section.

Eric Chang has done extensive research on the prepositions used in conjunction with Christ in the New Testament. His conclusion is that "in no instance of 'in Christ' and its variations is it ever necessary, grammatically or semantically, to render 'in Christ' as 'by Christ.'"[14]

Hence, just as God created the original physical universe with the first Adam in mind—with man being the reason, goal, and pinnacle of God's creative work, so the new creation has been brought into being with the second Adam in mind: with Christ being the reason, goal, and pinnacle of a new humanity, the people of God ("the church," v. 18). In God's new order, all things were inaugurated or created for Christ, just as all things continue to be created through Christ (perfect tense—ongoing) and all things belong to us in Christ (1 Cor. 3:22; 2 Cor. 4:15). If anyone is in Christ, he or she is a new creation; "the new creation has come" (2 Cor. 5:17).

"He is before all things" (v. 17). By assuming that "before" means prior to in time and "all things" refers to the initial creation, Trinitarians interpret this as a statement of Christ's personal preexistence. But while the Greek (*pro*) can mean "before or prior to" in time, its more common meaning is prior to in position or rank[15] (e.g., James 5:12; 1 Pet. 4:8).

This certainly fits the immediate context better, where Christ is "head of the body, the church," and Paul's crescendo builds to his climactic statement: "so that in everything he might have the supremacy." Of significance is the present tense of the verb used here. Paul doesn't say Christ was before all things, referring to a historical past state, but rather he refers to the present and ongoing state of affairs in God's new created order: "the kingdom of the Son he loves" (Col. 1:13).

---

14. Chang, *The Only Perfect Man*, 479.

15. BDAG.

Titus 2:13

> While we wait for the blessed hope—the appearing of the
> glory of our great God and Savior, Jesus Christ.

Interpretative bias causes many translations (as here in the NIV) to change the position of the pronoun "our" in the Greek text and place a comma after "Savior" in order to infer that Jesus is God. The most ancient manuscripts and translations, however, retain the original grammatical sense, where "our" refers to "savior." Hence: "...the appearing of the glory of the great God, and our Savior Jesus Christ." This is also consistent with the translation of every other occurrence of "our Savior" in this letter (1:3, 4; 2:10, 13; 3:4, 6).

The shifting of the pronoun was justified under the controversial "Granville Sharp Rule," named after its creator in the late-eighteenth century. Without going into the explanation of this rule, its validity is highly suspect[16] due to the fact that...

a. It was unknown to previous Greek linguists.

b. Granville Sharp admitted it was introduced to support Trinitarian Christology.

c. No respected scholar of koine Greek has ever vouched for its credibility.

d. In any case, it would not apply in this instance, where personal names or titles are an exception to the "rule."

This verse simply expresses the consistent teaching of the New Testament, that Jesus' second coming will be with, and in the glory of, God his Father (e.g., Matt. 16:27; 24:30; 25:31; Mark 8:38; 16:27-28; 2 Cor. 4:6).

Hebrews 1

> In the past God spoke to our ancestors through the
> prophets at many times and in various ways, but in these

---

16. Calvin Winstanley, *A Vindication of Certain Passages in the Common English Version of the New Testament: Addressed to Granville Sharp, Esq,* 2nd ed. (Cambridge: Cambridge University Press, 1819), 39–44.

> last days he has spoken to us by his Son, whom he appointed heir of all things, and through whom also he made the universe. The Son is the radiance of God's glory and the exact representation of his being, sustaining all things by his powerful word. After he had provided purification for sins, he sat down at the right hand of the Majesty in heaven. So he became as much superior to the angels as the name he has inherited is superior to theirs. (vv. 1-4)

This introduction presents a high and exalted view of Jesus. In fact, there are strong parallels between Hebrews 1:1-3 and the Colossians passage we have already examined:

- Both speak of the revelatory function of Jesus as the "image" or "representation" of God.
- Jesus is presented as heir, or the firstborn.
- His position of supremacy is highlighted.
- His upholding and sustaining power in God's kingdom is declared.
- His role of inaugurating the new creation is emphasized.

This last point needs to be stressed, as once again it sets the context. In verse 2, we read that through Jesus, God (literally) "made the ages" (*aionas*). Many versions translate this phrase as "created the universe," even though this rendering is without literary precedent. In the Bible, the Greek word *aion* never refers to the material creation. On the contrary, it is a spiritual concept.

There are two principal ages in salvation history—this age and the age to come—both converging and diverging at the pivotal point of the arrival of the Messiah (Matt. 12:32; Eph. 1:21). These correspond to the two covenants which are discussed at length later in the letter to the Hebrews: the "first covenant" and the "new covenant" (Heb. 8:7-8). *Yahweh* is the king of the ages (1 Tim. 1:17), who initiates and fulfills, through Christ, his eternal plan of salvation for mankind.

Note that Jesus is the "appointed" heir (not the inherent one), with an "inherited" name and conferred position (v. 4)—the agent "through whom" God is bringing about his new creation. This accords beautifully with Paul's statements in 1 Corinthians 8:4-6 and Colossians 1:14-18, which we've already examined.

The next statement, "The Son is the radiance of God's glory and the exact representation of his being" (v. 3), aligns with Paul's statements in 2 Corinthians 4: "God's glory displayed in the face of Christ" (v. 6b); "the glory of Christ, who is the image of God" (v. 4b). "All things" in God's new creation are being sustained by Jesus' powerful word, reflecting Colossians 1:17: "in him all things hold together."

The writer then quotes several Old Testament texts from the LXX to clearly present Jesus' exalted position, which is "at the right hand of the Majesty in heaven" (v. 3) and "much superior to the angels" (v. 4):

- Angels are "ministering spirits" (v. 14), whereas Jesus is God's unique son (v. 5).
- The angels will worship the Son (v. 6).
- The angels are servants (vv. 7, 14) but the Son is God's exalted king who will reign over an eternal kingdom (vv. 8-13).

By the way, verse 8 is a quote from Psalm 45, which is acknowledged by Bible scholars as an "ascension psalm," referring to Israel's king as God's anointed representative. The "God" title here should be viewed in this sense. Note that this human majesty has a God over him (v. 9). This is another example of the flexibility of the title "God" (*Elohim*) in Hebrew understanding and application.

Hebrews 1:10-13 is a challenging passage.[17] It reads as though Jesus is addressed as God, as the one who brought about the creation of the world: "In the beginning, Lord, you laid the foundations of the earth, and the heavens are the work of your hands" (v. 10).

However, it must be understood that...

- The author is quoting from the LXX, the Greek translation,

---

17. For a more detailed discussion, see Anthony Buzzard, *Jesus was Not a Trinitarian: a Call to Return to the Creed of Jesus* (Fayetteville, GA: Restoration Fellowship, 2007), 418-424.

not the Hebrew Scriptures. In this psalm these two texts differ significantly. A couple of the words have the same Hebrew consonants, which, when read with different vowel settings (added later), lead to two distinct interpretations.

- The LXX text has *Yahweh* addressing a messianic Lord, inviting him to initiate the founding of heaven and earth, a new political order in Israel, as we see in Isaiah's prophecy (Isa. 51:16).
- Although written in the past tense (as often with prophecy), this looks to the future age of God's coming kingdom— "the world to come, about which we are speaking" (Heb. 2:5). He is referring to the new creation, which Christ inaugurated upon his ascension (Heb. 9:11) and has yet to be culminated.
- The LXX being referenced by the author serves his intent precisely, as he seeks to convey the superiority of Christ over angels, because he is the founder of the coming messianic kingdom. We need to keep in mind this context. The key point being made is Christ's exalted position over angelic beings. The author is not trying to prove that Jesus is God, which he could have easily stated if he believed it.
- In verses 11—12, the author contrasts the permanency of the Messiah with the transient creation: "They will perish, but you remain...you remain the same, and your years will never end." This is not declaring that Jesus has always existed, but rather that his person and position are ongoing, unending, and unchanging. The same thought is expressed towards the end of the letter: "Jesus Christ is the same yesterday and today and forever" (Heb. 13:8).

Hence, verses 10-13, as a quote from Psalm 102, elaborate on the eternal reign of the king and must be read in their eschatological context—the coming messianic age of God's kingdom. The psalm speaks of this future kingdom to be established. It is a prophecy that is "written for a future generation, that a people not yet created may praise the LORD" (Ps. 102:18). As the writer to the Hebrews goes on to say: "It is not to angels that he has subjected the world to come, about which we are speaking" (2:5).

Chapter 2 of Hebrews maintains the distinction between "God, for whom and through whom everything exists" (v. 10) and Jesus, a "son of man" (v. 6), who has shared in our human condition (v. 14). Christ has been "appointed heir of all things" (1:2) and "crowned with glory and honor because he suffered death" (2:9). God has made "the pioneer of their salvation perfect through what he suffered" (2:10). If Jesus were already Almighty God, he wouldn't have needed to be perfected or appointed or to become superior (1:4). He would already have been these things.

1 Peter 1:10-11

> Concerning this salvation, the prophets, who spoke of the grace that was to come to you, searched intently and with the greatest care, trying to find out the time and circumstances to which the Spirit of Christ in them was pointing when he predicted the sufferings of the Messiah and the glories that would follow.

Some Trinitarians assume that the "Spirit of Christ" at work in the Old Testament prophets is a reference to Jesus' pre-incarnate spiritual state—his existence in the Spirit prior to his birth. However, such an interpretation is scripturally unsupported:

- Paul makes it clear that Adam existed before Christ (1 Cor. 15:45-49).
- The term "Spirit of Christ" (or "Spirit of Jesus," e.g., Acts 16:7) is not found in the Old Testament; it only appears in the New Testament after Jesus' resurrection and glorification.
- There is "one Spirit" (Eph. 4:4) variously designated according to the context and function the spirit performs. Hence, here it is not the Spirit which is Christ, but the spirit concerning the things of Christ—that is, fulfilling what the prophets discerned and revealed (Acts 3:18).

- There is a translation bias in this verse, where the Spirit of Christ is referred to as "he." No third person masculine pronoun occurs here in the Greek text.
- Peter's context is about prophetic inspiration, not about a supposed preexistent "spirit" Jesus.[18]

18. For verses not covered in this appendix, see John W. Schoenheit, Mark H. Graeser, and John A. Lynn, *One God & One Lord : Reconsidering the Cornerstone of the Christian Faith* (Indianapolis: Christian Educational Services, 2000); John Wilson, *Scripture Proofs and Scriptural Illustrations of Unitarianism* (1846; repr., London: Forgotten Books, 2017).

RESOURCES

Anthony Buzzard
www.focusonthekingdom.org

Kegan Chandler
www.burieddeepblog.wordpress.com

Christian Disciples Church
www.christiandiscipleschurch.org

Sean Finnegan
www.restitutio.org
www.christianmonotheism.com

J. Dan Gill
www.21stcr.org

Bill Schlegel
www.onegodreport.com

Dustin Smith
www.biblicalunitarianpodcast.podbean.com

Dale Tuggy
www.trinities.org/blog

Web Resources:
www.angelfire.com/space/thegospeltruth/trinity.html
www.thebiblejesus.com
www.biblicalunitarian.com
www.unitarianchristianalliance.org
www.christbeforecreeds.com

Bibliography

Bailey, Kenneth E. *Jesus Through Middle Eastern Eyes: Cultural Studies in the Gospels*. Downers Grove, IL: InterVarsity Press, 2008.

Bainton, Roland H. *Hunted Heretic: The Life and Death of Michael Servetus 1511-1553*. Rev. ed. Providence: Blackstone Editions, 2005.

Bauer, Walter, Frederick Danker, William Arndt, and F. Wilbur Gingrich. *A Greek-English Lexicon of the New Testament and Other Early Christian Literature*. 3rd ed. Chicago: University of Chicago Press, 2002.

BeDuhn, Jason David. *Truth in Translation*. Lanham, MD: University Press of America, 2003.

Buzzard, Anthony and Charles Hunting. *The Doctrine of the Trinity: Christianity's Self-inflicted Wound*. Lanham, MD: International Scholars Publications, 1998.

Brown, Colin, ed. *New International Dictionary of New Testament Theology*. 4 vols. Grand Rapids, MI: Zondervan, 1986.

Carslake, Graham. *DNA of the Churches of Christ Movement*. Miami: Xlibris, 2014.

Chang, Eric H.H. *The Only Perfect Man: The Glory of God in the Face of Jesus Christ*. 2nd ed. Edited by Bentley Chan. Charleston, SC: Christian Disciples Church, 2017.

The Only True God: A Study of Biblical Monotheism. Miami: Xlibris, 2009.

Deuble, Greg S. *They Never Told Me This in Church!: A Call to Read the Bible with New Eyes*. 2nd ed. Fayetteville, GA: Restoration Fellowship, 2010.

Dunn, James D. G. *Christology in the Making*. London: SCM Press, 1989.

Erickson, Millard J. *God in Three persons: A Contemporary Interpretation of the Trinity*. Grand Rapids, MI: Baker Books, 1995.

Foster, Douglas A., Anthony L. Dunnavant, Paul M. Blowers, and D. Newell Williams, eds. *The Encyclopedia of the Stone-Campbell Movement*. Grand Rapids, MI: Eerdmans, 2004.

González, Justo L. *The Story of Christianity*. Peabody, MA: Hendrickson Publishers, 2001.

Hach, Robert. *Possession and Persuasion; The Rhetoric of Christian Faith*. Miami: Xlibris, 2001.

Hanson, A. T. *The Image of the Invisible God*. London: SCM Press, 1982.

Hanson, R. P. C. *The Search for the Christian Doctrine of God*. Grand Rapids, MI: Baker Academic, 2005.

Hefele, Karl Joseph. *A History of the Councils of the Church: form the Original Documents, to the close of the Second Council of Nicaea A.D. 787*. Eugene, OR: Wipf & Stock Pub, 2007.

Hopkins, Richard R. *How Greek Philosophy Corrupted the Christian Concept of God*. Bountiful, UT: Horizon Publishers, 2005.

Kittel, Gerhard, Gerhard Friedrich, and Geoffrey W. Bromiley. *Theological Dictionary of the New Testament: Abridged in One Volume; A Greek-English Lexicon of the New Testament and Other Early Christian Literature*. Grand Rapids, MI: Eerdmans, 1985.

Küng, Hans. *Christianity: Its Essence and History*. London: SCM Press, 1995.

Kuhn, Thomas S. *The Structure of Scientific Revolutions*. 3rd ed. Chicago: The University of Chicago Press, 1996.

Kuschel, Karl-Josef. *Born Before all Time? The Dispute over Christ's Origin*. New York: Crossroad, 1992.

Lamson, Alvan. *The Church of the First Three Centuries*. 2nd ed. Boston: Walker, Fuller, and Company, 1865.

Matthews, W. R. *God in Christian Experience*. London: James Nisbet and Co., 1930.

Metzger, Bruce and Michael D. Coogan, eds. *Oxford Companion to the Bible*. Oxford: Oxford University Press, 1993.

Murphy, Roland. *The Tree of Life: An Exploration of Biblical Wisdom Literature*. Grand Rapids, MI: Eerdmans, 2002.

Percival, Henry R., ed. and trans. *The Seven Ecumenical Councils*. Nicene and Post-Nicene Fathers: 2nd series, vol. 14. Edited by Philip Schaff and Henry Wace. 1900. Reprint, Peabody, MA: Hendrickson Publishers, 2004.

Rubenstein, Richard E. *When Jesus Became God: The Epic Fight Over Christ's Divinity in the last Days of Rome*. New York: Harcourt Brace and Co., 1999.

Smail, Thomas A. *The Forgotten Father*. Grand Rapids, MI: Eerdmans, 1981.

Snaith, N. H. *The Distinctive Ideas of the Old Testament*. Philadelphia: Westminster Press, 1946.

Thayer, Joseph Henry. *Greek–English Lexicon of the New Testament*. New York: Harper & Brothers, 1889.

Tuggy, Dale and Christopher M. Date. *Is Jesus Human and Not Divine?* Warrendale, PA: Areopagus Books, 2020.

Trinities. Dale Tuggy. https://trinities.org/blog/.

Werblowsky, R. J. Zwi. *Encyclopedia of The Jewish Religion*. Rev. ed. Edited by Geoffrey Widoger. London: Phoenix House, 1996.

Williams, E. Lyall. *Living Responsibly*. Glen Iris, Victoria: Vital Publications, 1976.

Winstanley, Calvin. *A Vindication of Certain Passages in the Common English Version of the New Testament: Addressed to Granville Sharp, Esq.* 2nd ed. Cambridge: Cambridge University Press, 1819.

Wright, N. T. *Surprised by Hope: Rethinking Heaven, the Resurrection, and the Mission of the Church*. 2008. Reprint, New York: HarperOne, 2008.

Printed in Great Britain
by Amazon